INNER PEACE

ACHIEVING SELF-ESTEEM

THROUGH PRAYER

INNER PEACE

ACHIEVING SELF-ESTEEM
THROUGH PRAYER

First published 1999
ISBN 1-56871-189-1 hardcover
Copyright © 1999 by Yisroel Roll
Revised edition 2001
All rights reserved

Phototypeset at Targum Press

Published by:
Targum Press Inc.
22700 W. Eleven Mile Rd.
Southfield, Mich. 48034
targum@elronet.co.il

Distributed by:
Feldheim Publishers
200 Airport Executive Park
Nanuet, N.Y. 10954

Distributed in Israel by:
Targum Press Ltd.
POB 43170
Jerusalem 91430

Printed in Israel

This book contains the name of God and must be treated with respect.

The full Name of God has a special sancity. To avoid any possible desecration Jewish tradition substitutes the letter ק (transliterated as the letter "k") for the letter ה (transliterated as an "h"). In this book, we have followed this traditional usage, except in the actual prayers themselves, when God's Name is spelled out correctly.

Nachman Bulman   נחמן בולמן
ישיבת אור שמח — ירושלים

Erev Pesach 5759-1999

A striking new work on prayer, "Inner Peace," by Rabbi Yisroel Roll, has been brought to my attention for review.

The author has won wide esteem for his inspiring effect on many who seek access to the wellsprings of Torah life.

Rabbi Roll helps siddur-words resonate in the psyche and emotions of Jews who do not initially connect with the siddur-words and images, even though they read those words in print. He writes unpretentiously, but from heart to heart. He awakens the elemental chords of the music of the Jewish heart.

The transcending words of every passage and section in our prayer service become a process of self-discovery. Not theology or philosphy or legal theory alone speak to us in Rabbi Roll's "Inner Peace," but a record of living encounter between God and Israel unfolds before us.

הכותב למען כבוד התורה עבד לעבדי ה׳ בשם העומדים לפניו בתפילה

נחמן בולמן
ירושלם ת״ו

לעלוי נשמת

This book is dedicated to the memory of

העדיל הענא בת העניך מרדכי ז״ל   יצחק בן יעקב ז״ל

Hazel and Cyril Symons, *z"l*

Dedicated by their son,
Jonathan Symons.

לעלוי נשמת

In memory of my maternal grandparents

דוד אבא בן יהודה לייב הכהן ז״ל
רבקה בת ישראל ז״ל
מגזע ישראל חריף מסאטנוב זצ״ל, מחבר ספר תפארת ישראל

David Abba and Rivka Huberman, *z"l*
who loved Torah and were *gomlei chasadim.*

In memory of my paternal grandparents

חיים יהודה בן נתן נטע ז״ל
and
אסתר בת שלמה הכהן ז״ל
Julius and Erna Roll, *z"l,*
who lived Torah values and
communal leadership.

CONTENTS

ACKNOWLEDGMENTS

I would like to express my gratitude to the following individuals whose help contributed significantly to the publication of this book:

Rabbi Dr. Dovid Gottlieb, who reviewed and edited three drafts of the manuscript and discussed the issues with me over many hours in great detail. His Torah insights and thoughts are woven into every page of this book.

Rabbi Dr. Abraham Twerski, for his review of the manuscript and for his encouragement.

Dayan Chanoch Ehrentreu, Rosh Beis Din of the London Beis Din for his *chizuk*, guidance, and inspiration. Harav Nachman Bulman, for always making time for his *talmidim* and for the depth of his wisdom and guidance. Rabbi Yaakov Bradpiece, of Ohr Somayach, Jerusalem, for his ongoing guidance and *chizuk*. Rabbi Elozor Robinson of Toronto for his inspiration and wise counsel.

Rabbi Danny Kirsch, my first *chavrusah* in London, for his *chizuk* and friendship and for discussing many of the ideas found in this book. My brother-in-law, Rabbi Menachem Nissel of Jerusalem, for sparking my imagination to go beyond the possible. Rabbi Shlomo Mernick of Toronto, for his *chizuk* and encouragement.

Dr. Michael Sinclair, who first recruited me to join the New West End Synagogue in London, England. His vision and support facilitated many of the experiences related in this book that occurred while I served as Rabbi to the New West End Synagogue community. Alan Gainsford and John Bodie, Honorary Officers of the New West End Synagogue, who supported my initiatives and synagogue projects.

Jonathan Symons of London and Gary Torgow of Detroit, for their friendship, advice, and support. Rabbi Malcolm Levine, Mordechai Mandelbaum, David Kutner, Ralph Levine, Harvey Brenman, Cyril Brenman and their families, of Toronto, for their friendship, open homes, and encouragement. Rabbi Shimon Kurland, Rabbi Joseph Kaufman, Shlomie Ehrentreu, and Melech Simon, for their friendship and support.

Rabbi Moshe Dombey for believing in this project and for his professionalism throughout. Ita Olesker, Miriam Zakon, and D. Liff of Targum Press for their helpful ideas, editing, and input. Florie Cohen, who expertly typed the manuscript.

My parents, Walter and Shirley Roll of Montreal, for their support and encouragement and for inspiring me to follow my dreams. My in-laws, Larry and Lorraine Brown of Memphis, for their support and encouragement. My sister, Mrs. Loretta Rubin of Montreal, for her review of the manuscript and helpful ideas, and my brother, Malcolm Roll, for his encouragement.

My children, Rivka Malka, Dovid Simcha, Rina Esther, Yehudah Yehonason, and Channah Shifra, for their wonderful inspiration.

And finally, my wife, Julie, who makes my journey toward inner peace an exciting adventure.

Yisroel Roll

Iyar 5761

FOREWORD

by Rabbi Dr. Dovid Gottlieb

Inner Peace: Achieving Self-Esteem through Prayer gives a unique perspective on prayer and all of Torah life which is greatly lacking in our generation. Many books are available in English explaining the idea and the text of prayer, but they do not portray its central place in the development of a Torah life.

Torah literature is replete with works expounding Torah law, philosophy, translation and commentary of central texts, history, and evaluation of contemporary issues and communal concerns. But descriptions of how Torah life *feels*, what it means to *experience* the world in Torah terms, are rare. Is it ever appropriate to feel "down"? How does trust in God affect our emotions in a crisis? What is the joy felt in the service of God, or at a *simchah*? What are the emotions which we do feel, and should feel, when we strive to grow closer to God through spiritual development? What emotions does the Torah catalyze in our relationships with our family, friends, co-workers, neighbors? This is an area of Torah which is greatly neglected. Rabbi Roll has brought a wealth of Torah sources to bear on this crucial subject.

Many will benefit from his groundbreaking effort, and it is to be hoped that other authors will follow his example to develop this subject even further.

In the day-to-day experience of Torah living and conversation there is another missing subject: God. One *baal teshuvah* who came to Torah observance after experience in another religion observed that while he heard a great deal in Torah circles about values, philosophy, law, family, spirituality, growth, history, beauty, etc., God was rarely mentioned. There may be a fear of sounding too "fundamentalist," too "primitive," by speaking about God. Or the subject may be too personal to share with others. But the result is the loss of the reality of God as a living presence. The goal of a Jew's life is *deveikus*: "I have placed God before me continuously." We must live in continuous conscious relationship with God. Speaking of God expresses this living reality. If our reticence inhibits our expression of this experience of relationship with God, we, our families, and our community are spiritually impoverished. *Inner Peace* fills this need. Rabbi Roll speaks (what he calls) the "G" word throughout the book without hesitation. It is clear that he does so because for him God is a living reality. It is to be hoped that through reading this book the experience of God will be enhanced for others as well, and again that other authors will follow his lead.

Having known Rabbi Roll through his studies at Yeshivat Ohr Somayach, and having enjoyed sharing *kiruv* (outreach) efforts with him, it is an event of great personal joy and satisfaction to see his writing come to fruition and become available to the many Jews whose Torah lives will be immeasurably deepened by it.

FOREWORD

by Rabbi Dr. Abraham Twerski

Tefillah — the word for prayer — also has the meaning of bonding (see Rashi, Bereishis 30:8). Prayer can indeed bond: man with God, man with fellowman, and man with himself.

There are three themes that are prominent in prayer: *ahavah*, declaration of our love of God; *hoda'ah*, gratitude towards God; and *vidui*, confessing our wrongdoings to God. It is obvious that God, Who is absolute perfection, is not in need of our expressions of love, of gratitude, or of penitence. Clearly these are intended to elevate man spiritually and are primarily for our own betterment.

Think of how many relationships are shattered because of some people's inability or hesitance to express love and gratitude, or to admit one's mistakes. How many broken homes could have been preserved if the three magic phrases — I love you, I thank you, and I was wrong — would have been voiced more frequently. Whether between man and wife, or between friends, these three simple phrases can bind and reinforce a relationship.

The resistance to expressing love, gratitude, and remorse are in a large part due to lack of self-esteem. A person plagued by feelings of inferiority and unworthiness may feel incapable of being loved, hence he cannot love another. He may feel that being thankful to another person for a favor received constitutes indebtedness, and he does not wish to feel obligated or beholden to others. Finally, a person with low self-esteem may feel threatened by the recognition, let alone the admission, that he has done wrong.

Because God is all supreme and because He is an abstraction, there may be less resistance to expressing our love for Him, our gratitude to Him, and our remorse for our mistakes. However, once we allow ourselves to verbalize these ideas to God, once we hear ourselves say these words to Him, it may lessen our resistance and hesitancy to say them to our friends or to those whom we love.

Prayer is thus an integral component of self-esteem, and conversely, self-esteem enhances the quality of prayer. That prayer can actually help us achieve an identity is explicitly stated by the Psalmist, "I am a prayer" (Tehillim 109:4). Thus, by binding man to God, prayer also bonds man with fellowman, and bonds one with oneself.

Rabbi Roll has called upon the works of our Torah scholars throughout our history to clarify the relevance of prayer to self-esteem and their interrelationship. We are indebted to him for helping us make our prayer more meaningful, more uplifting, and more effective in bringing us closer to others and to ourselves as well.

Whenever your inner or outer life points out to you the need for acquiring enlightenment and strength, a sanctified will and an inner peace, you should withdraw from the bustle of life towards God: and in prayer flowing from your inner self, gather these treasures for life before His countenance.

Rabbi Samson Raphael Hirsch,
Horeb, Avodah 114:697

Preface

THE "G" WORD

Western society has a problem with the "G" word. God. There, I said it. Modern people usually associate discussions about God with "fundamentalism " and a "Middle Ages" mentality. Few rational people would consider discussions about letting God into their lives as "politically correct." "Too heavy, too religious," they would say. Conventional wisdom says that self-sufficient man no longer needs the man-made "crutch" of God or religion. He relies only on progress, which is basically himself.

Religion, in general, and prayer, in particular, have been looked upon with skepticism. Modern psychologists consider religion a function of man's creative imagination, something man has conjured up because he "needs" religion and prayer to calm his psyche and to make sense of the pressures of life.

Young professionals with whom I study have confided to me that initially they became interested in spiritual life because they were seeking an improvement in their otherwise superficial, day to day, 8 A.M. to 8 P.M. existence (the 9 to 5 workday is a thing of the past). The "post-yuppie" generation has achieved relative financial success and lives a fast-paced life surrounded by modern comforts. They now seek, however, to improve the quality of their lives. They seek meaning and purpose — perhaps a luxury that their parents and grandparents had little time to pursue while they sought to survive two World Wars and the Depression.

A member of my synagogue, a young family man who runs a highly successful travel business, comes to our shul's morning services. He is not particularly observant, but he has told me that he finds the forty-five minutes in the morning gives him a moment of "personal space" to collect his thoughts and to focus his mind. He confided that the morning service is like an island of time — an oasis of spiritual privacy that gives him the spiritual strength to face the pressures of the coming day.

This is one valid level of prayer. This orientation, however, can form the foundation for an even deeper and more inspiring level of prayer.

Many who embark upon the Jewish spiritual adventure find that the Torah way of life, and in particular *tefillah*, helps them activate their creative energies and build an inner sense of tranquility and balance. Torah philosophy, with its emphasis on self-awareness, personal growth, and character development, generates a feeling of optimism, self-confidence, and personal vision. While all this is true, it can leave us with the false impression that the prayer experience, and Torah in general, is merely a strategy for a "self-help" program. The Torah and prayer can be mistaken for a "do it yourself," best-selling psychology book by a popular, self-help psychologist. Although there is personal growth through Torah, the thinking Jew must graduate to "*avodah*," service of God, as his real connection to God.

This "graduation" requires a shift of focus from the personal benefits one receives from Torah and prayer to the concept of "working for" or "following the Will" of God. We serve Hashem not merely because our prayers allow us to get to know ourselves better, but because they allow us to get to know God better.

We serve Hashem and His Torah standards ultimately because God is the True Standard as revealed to Moshe Rabbeinu and *Klal Yisrael* on Mount Sinai. Hashem reached down into the world at Sinai and Israel reached up to Him. Jews today continue this process of reaching up to God through Torah (Torah study and the performance of the commandments), *avodah* (service of God through prayer), and *gemillus chassadim* (kind deeds).[1]

While going through this process of the service of Hashem, and in particular through *iyun tefillah* — absorption and understanding prayer — I can indeed grow and clarify who I am and where I am going. The development and growth of my character and personality to rise to God's standards is, in and of itself, an expression of my service of God. I serve God by working on my character and by becoming the best person I can be, using the Torah and Halachah as the yardstick with which to measure my progress.

Deveikus — connection to the Source (Hashem) — is the ultimate pathway and goal. Feeling the warmth and closeness of walking along God's path gives me a sense of direction and wholeness in the realization that I am doing not only "the right thing" but "the real thing."

NOTES

1. *Pirkei Avos* 1:2.

Prayer is a personal experience. Whenever the word "I" is used in this book it is not the author speaking. Put yourself into the "I" and read it as if you are speaking. Then you can begin to embark upon a personal journey toward self-esteem through prayer.

Introduction

FROM SELF-AWARENESS TO SELF-ESTEEM

I know that I am required by Jewish Law "to get out of bed in the morning like a lion,"[1] but sometimes, I must confess, it does not happen. In fact, some days, I feel shattered and drained. The new day has dawned but my mind can't seem to connect with that adventurous feeling the sunrise is supposed to produce. I drag myself to our local community minyan, and something happens to my mood. The words of the morning davening lift me, move me, strengthen me. That is what this book is about.

I have found that there is a magical quality to the words of our prayers. Even if I am not quite paying attention to the words I am saying, a word or a phrase might catch my eye and inject me with renewed strength — I feel uplifted. There must be some power in these words. Imagine how I might feel if I actually applied my mind with *kavanah* (intention and concentration) upon the prayers. On the days I am "connected" and paying attention, I could actually be moved to a state of "inspired prayer."

Too many minyanim seem to be sending their prayers heavenward by fax or e-mail. A twenty-eight-minute executive minyan special, with one foot out the door and usually the whole mind focused on the morning's partners' meeting or conference call, is unlikely to inspire. True inspiration in the morning could get me in touch with my real "inner self." It could energize my self-concept as I relate to God and to those around me. But it takes an investment of effort, concentration, and pre-davening preparation, by reviewing the meaning of the words in evening study sessions, to place myself in a position to daven with *kavanah*.[2]

The prayers composed by the *Anshei Knesses HaGedolah*, among whom were the prophets Mordechai, Ezra, and Nechemiah, were designed to connect me with the Source. The Sages, in their wisdom and high levels of spiritual sensitivity gained through their Torah scholarship, knew *b'ruach hakodesh* (Divine inspiration) how to open the channels of communication and to connect with God. The words of the prayers can open my heart and focus my thoughts. Prayer can actually help me clarify the way I feel about myself and put my *neshamah* onto the correct frequency to receive the *berachah* (blessing) from the *breichah* (pool of blessing) that is Hashem.[3] All I need do is "tap in" to the flow of *berachah*. Prayer allows me to open the tap and initiate a meaningful relationship with God.

The prayers are not for God, however. Hashem does not need my prayers. He is already perfect, and nothing I can say can add to His perfection. The prayers allow me to clarify where I stand vis-à-vis Hashem. The prayer process can help me to get to know myself. It allows me some "quality time" to focus on my strengths and how I can develop them. It allows me to pinpoint my faults and weaknesses and gives me planning time to reflect on how I can grow and better myself.

When I pray to the Creator, I realize that I am part of God's universe, and that I am part of His plan for the world. I count in God's eyes. This realization can help me focus on my identity and allow me to work on and develop my self-esteem. The prayer process can put me in touch with my real self — my *neshamah* — and in turn can help me develop a positive and healthy self-image.

One of the main reasons for a "downer" morning and a low energy level is a lack of self-esteem. A negative self-image or self-concept can be the source of my lack of motivation and "get up and go." If I look at myself negatively or overly critically, this will lead to a lower than appropriate level of functioning.[4] My interpersonal relationships will suffer as will my day to day home and business performance. How can I relate well to others if I cannot relate positively to myself?

Only an open "give and take" relationship with God can give me a true sense of self. Why? God is *the* sole reality of the universe.[5] He is the First Cause and Prime Mover.[6] I owe my very existence to God. My next breath depends entirely upon Him. Without God, the Source and Sustainer of life, nothing could exist, even for an instant. When I appreciate and understand that I have been created *b'tzelem Elokim* (in the image of God), I can instill in my mind a sense of "belonging" in this world. I belong to God and thus have a place and a role to play in His universe. This means that by virtue of merely "being" I have worth. I don't have to "do" or to "accomplish" to have self-worth. I merely have to "be" in order to be worthy in God's eyes. When I come into contact

with the Life Force Itself through prayer, I become energized by a feeling of being "alive." Imagine if I was able to
carry this thought and feeling around with me in a vibrant
way all day long. It would energize every breath, thought,
and action with meaning and purpose.

God created me because He wants to give me the best
things in life. He wants me to get the most out of life. What is
the best life has to offer? God.[7] It is up to me to develop a
connection and relationship with God Himself. A connection
with my Source will energize the way I think about myself. It
will make me aware of my own space — my own reality in relation to the Ultimate Reality — God. It will create within me a
sense of "self" or self-awareness in that I "am" — in relation to
my God. Self-awareness must then be transformed into positive thinking about myself. Prayer is designed to do just that.
The prayer process can help me develop a more meaningful
relationship with God and thereby affirm my personal value
as an individual. By allowing me to focus on my strengths and
weaknesses, and my goals for personal growth in relation to
what God expects of me, prayer can help me develop positive
feelings about myself and thereby enhance my self-esteem.

Can I relate to God Himself? Yes. Not only can I — but I
am obligated to.

Let us illustrate. There is a story told of a man who once
saved the king's life. The king gave him three days to think
about the reward he wanted. As he approached the palace
gate on the third day, he had in mind to ask the king for a
castle filled with gold. As he entered the royal foyer filled
with its majestic gold furniture, he thought to himself: "Why
settle for one castle? I'll ask for two castles filled with
golden furniture." As he was led by the king's courtiers

through the state room and saw the golden table surrounded by one hundred golden chairs, he said to himself:
"Why should I settle for two castles? I will ask for three."
When he stood before the king who was seated on his
throne, which was surrounded by glistening golden eagles,
he thought to himself: "Why should I settle for three castles
when I can have everything?" So in response to the king's
question as to what he wanted, the man said: "Your Majesty,
as my reward I would like to marry your daughter."

Since God is the source of everything, why should we
settle for material well-being or any other thing of this
world? Let us ask to be connected to the King Himself.
There is no greater pleasure than a relationship with the
King. This is called *deveikus*, a cleaving, an embracing of
God Himself. There can be no greater pleasure than to em-
brace the Source of life and allow God to be our personal
King, strength, and support.

Let us now take a deeper look at some of the morning
prayers and see how a little understanding, and *kavanah*,
can allow the words to penetrate my *neshamah* and help develop my self-concept and, in turn, my self-worth.

NOTES

1. *Shulchan Aruch, Orach Chaim* 1:1.
2. Rabbi Shimon Pinkus, *Sha'arim BeTefillah* (Ofakim, Negev: 1993), ch. 1.
3. Rabbi Chaim of Volozhin, *Nefesh HaChaim, sha'ar alef.*
4. Abraham Twerski, *I am I* (New York: The Shaar Press, 1993), 10.
5. Rambam, *Hilchos Yesodei HaTorah*, 1:1–4.
6. Ibid., 1:5.
7. Rabbi Moshe Chaim Luzatto, *Derech Hashem*, part 1, ch. 7.

Chapter 1

ARISING IN THE MORNING

מודה אני
Waking Up Inspired

מוֹדֶה אֲנִי לְפָנֶיךָ, מֶלֶךְ חַי וְקַיָּם, שֶׁהֶחֱזַרְתָּ בִּי נִשְׁמָתִי בְּחֶמְלָה,
רַבָּה אֱמוּנָתֶךָ.

*I gratefully thank You, O living and eternal
King, for you have returned my soul to me, with
compassion — abundant is Your faithfulness.*

The first word a Jew says in the morning is *"modeh,"* which comes from the root word *"todah"* — meaning "thankfulness." I am thanking God for returning my soul to me this morning. After all, He didn't have to. He has, in His wisdom, given me another chance to further my life goal of working toward my potential by presenting me with a new day of spectacular adventure.

Adventure? The first thought that usually enters my mind in the morning is "I can't believe it's morning already." (Straight denial mode.) Can't I hit the snooze bar and delay this adventure for a few more hours? The key to waking up inspired is understanding the word *"modeh."*

The first ingredient for any successful relationship is acknowledgment and recognition of the other party as an entity apart from myself. Recognizing God as a real, rather than as a theoretical entity, puts me into a mind-set to begin relating to Him directly. This acknowledgment, found in the word *"modeh,"* brings with it a sense of humility and gratitude which reminds me that I did not create myself, rather I get my energy from a Source outside of myself. That Source is my Creator, and when I say *modeh* I acknowledge and thank Him for re-creating me this morning. When I say *modeh* I am responding to God's challenge, which is nothing less than to re-create my self-image.

The second word a Jew says in the morning is *"ani"* — "I." After I acknowledge God as my Source when I say *modeh* — thank you — I can then begin to personally relate to God. This word *"ani"* creates within me a self-awareness — an appreciation of my own existence. I actually have an opportunity to relate to the Chairman of the Board. I can relate to Him directly, I don't even have to make an appointment with His secretary. No waiting, a direct line. All I have to do is pick up the red phone: *"Modeh ani* — I thank You."

The first person in the Torah to say "thank you" and who really understood the meaning of gratefulness was our matriarch Leah. Upon the birth of her fourth son, Yehudah, she said: "This time I shall give thanks to God, and she called him Yehudah."[1]

The root word of Yehudah is *"todah"* — thankfulness. Rashi, commenting on this verse, states: *"This time I shall give thanks to God...*because I have received more than my portion, therefore it is incumbent upon me to thank Him."

Leah was a prophetess. She knew Yaakov was to have four wives and twelve sons. Thus, she calculated that each wife would rightfully bear Yaakov three sons. Upon the birth of her fourth son, she realized that she had received a blessing of one child more than her entitlement. So she said thank you, because she felt gratitude for gratuitously receiving more than she deserved.

Leah grasped the concept that she owed a special debt of gratitude for receiving an undeserved, free gift of an "extra" son. She then carried the thought to its logical conclusion. In essence, every child she was granted was a gift from God. She had as little to do with the birth of her fourth child as she had with her first three. Not only did the gratuitous gift of bearing more than her allotted share of Yaakov's children deserve a "thank you" to God, but *everything* she was given by God deserved and was an opportunity to communicate her thanks to Him.

Most people have accepted Western terminology claiming a person's "right to life." The pro-life movement speaks of a fetus' right to life. The American Declaration of Independence speaks of the "right to life, liberty, and the pursuit of happiness." A "right" may be thought of as "freedom of action which others are morally bound to respect and protect." In Judaism, we speak not of "rights" but of "mitzvos" — duties and obligations. Rights arise out of a deserving act or deed, which causes one to earn the right to a reward. Our brief yet traumatic journey down the birth canal can hardly be seen as our earning our place in this world. As far as I can remember, I didn't have too much choice whether I wanted to make the journey. My life was handed to me at birth, on a silver platter. It was an undeserved, gratuitous gift of God in partnership with my parents.

I don't have a right to life. Just because I have been here until now does not guarantee that I will be here ten seconds from now. God is not obligated to continue sustaining me in life just because He has done so until now. He keeps me alive out of pure altruistic love for me — His creature, His child. Every breath, if it is measured and deeply appreciated, can infuse my life with meaning and awe.

As I conclude these opening words of *Modeh Ani* I make an incredible statement: "Abundant is Your faithfulness." Hold it! Shouldn't I be saying "abundant is *my* faithfulness"? Isn't it my obligation to have faith in God? What's all this about God's faithfulness? The truth is that Hashem does have faith — in me. God believes in me. He proved it by restoring my life to me this morning, precisely because He does have faith that I can succeed in developing myself and do my share in furthering Hashem's plan for the world, today. Let's have none of this false modesty stuff. Hashem has faith in me, so don't I have a right to have faith in myself?

אלקי נשמה
The Real Me

אֱלֹהַי, נְשָׁמָה שֶׁנָּתַתָּ בִּי טְהוֹרָה הִיא...כָּל זְמַן שֶׁהַנְּשָׁמָה בְּקִרְבִּי,
מוֹדֶה אֲנִי לְפָנֶיךָ, ה' אֱלֹהַי...

My God, the neshamah (soul) which You bestowed in me is pure...so long as the neshamah is within me I give thanks to You, Hashem, my God...

I am bigger than my *neshamah*. When I say, "the *neshamah* which You bestowed in me" I am saying that my identity, the "me," is comprised of my physical body and my *neshamah*.[2] The *berachah* that immediately precedes this one is *Asher Yatzar*, which thanks God for the wonders of my physical being. Then I follow onto *Elokai Neshamah* dealing with my soul. The "real me" is the totality and the integration of my body and soul.[3] It is the point where my body and soul meet. It is my *nekudah hapenimis* — my central core.

When God created Adam, the first man, the Torah says: "And He blew into his nostrils the spirit of life."[4] God takes part of Himself, the Source of life, the Generator of all life, and without diminishing anything of Himself, implants within me a *neshamah* — a life force. This life force is known as *"chelek Eloka mima'al"* — "a portion of God from above." God is the *Ein Sof* — the Infinite — and He has placed a spark of His Infinite Energy into me, as my soul. I therefore have Godliness pulsing within my very being. The goal is to "meet," to get to know and to get in touch with, the Godliness within me. If I could activate that connection I would be tapped into the Infinite Source of life itself. Think of it — constant renewed energy, perpetual rechargeable batteries. No possibility of burnout.

וְאַתָּה עָתִיד לִטְּלָהּ מִמֶּנִּי, וּלְהַחֲזִירָהּ בִּי לֶעָתִיד לָבֹא.

You will eventually take it from me and restore it to me in the time to come.

The Talmud[5] tells a story of a blind man and a lame man who could not accomplish anything as a result of their respective handicaps. The blind man said to the lame man,

"Why don't you get on my shoulders. I will be your legs and you will be my eyes." They walked into the king's orchard and ate of the king's fruit. They thus committed a transgression. The lame man then got down off the blind man's shoulders. When confronted with the transgression, each said: "I could not possibly have done anything wrong." The blind man said, "I cannot see." The lame man said, "I cannot walk." The king then put the lame man back onto the shoulders of the blind man — and judged them together.

The Talmud provides the *nimshal* — the message of this story. I may say before God: "It wasn't me! I could not have failed to follow Your instructions." My *neshamah* will say, "I cannot walk without a body." My body will say, "I cannot 'see,' since I am like a lump of clay without a soul." God will then restore my soul to my body at the end of days, and judge my body and soul together as one.

The real me is a combination of my body and soul. My soul cannot accomplish anything unless it is within my body. The body cannot move without the *neshamah*. It is my life's goal to integrate body and soul.[6] This means that I can spiritualize the physical components of my being by acting in a moral and ethical fashion in accordance with the Torah's instructions. God put two disparate, opposite forces into one entity: the physical side of man as well as the spiritual dimension. They are placed into one human form. Whenever I feel that warm feeling of inner tranquility, peace, and contentedness, from having performed an act of *chessed*, for example, it is because for that moment I have succeeded in integrating body and soul. The feeling of *"geshmack"* (the Yiddish word for delight) is one of the warmest, most energized feelings in the world. It is a moment of unity of body and soul. It is a moment of *deveikus* — connecting the Godliness within me to its Source — an embrace of God.

In the performance of mitzvos we can see this idea take shape. The tefillin placed on the arm represent the "outstretched arm" of God, and in human terms represent the deeds and actions of man. The head tefillin represent the mind and soul cleaving to God. I accomplish this by using my mind (my *sechel*) and my *neshamah*, which is centered in the mind, in the service of Hashem. When I put on the arm tefillin and then the head tefillin, I am attempting to unify my deeds (symbolized by the arm tefillin) with my thoughts (symbolized by the head tefillin). My body and soul can be aligned in a common effort to serve Hashem. If my thoughts guide my deeds in one purposeful direction, I can be placed on track toward fulfilling my potential — achieving my mission or goal in life.

When I connect with God's will by following the Torah, then I am on the same spiritual "frequency" as God. When I fulfill the mitzvos I am connected to the underlying grain and flow of the universe. I am close to God. God is perfect, the ultimate in goodness. When I am close to God, I am energized. When I am disconnected from God's will — by failing to follow the Torah — then I am distanced or estranged from God. This is the meaning of the word "*ra*," evil. "*Ra*" comes from the word "*raua*," meaning shaky.

When I am on shaky or unfirm ground, I am "off the track" and therefore distant from God. The Torah[7] states: "*Vayomer eilai Hashem, asher hishalachti lefanav...*" — "God replied to me: Hashem, before Whom I have walked..." Rashi[8] comments that "while Noach required

God's support, Avraham walked before God as he strengthened himself, and walked [before God] purely of his own
choice and volition." When I am not following God's will I
am *ra* — on shaky ground. My goal is to get on track, "to
walk before God." Avraham worked on himself and placed
himself "in the pathway of God's Truth," on God's spiritual
wavelength. If I get close enough to God to be sufficiently inspired, then I graduate to walking before God, to do His will
in perfecting the world. My task is to place myself, body and
soul, deeds and thoughts, into harmony with God's will.

וְאַתָּה מְשַׁמְּרָה בְקִרְבִּי.

You preserve it within me.

This soul that You, God, placed within me, is preserved
and guided by You, God. This is the concept of *hashgachah
pratis* — Divine Providence. God is within me and speaks to
me through the *neshamah*. There is a direct link between the
world of *atzilus* (the fourth dimension of the spiritual world
from which the soul emanates)[9] and the soul as it resides
within me in this world. Through the events that happen to
me, God is guiding, directing, and teaching me. The events
that happen to me are arranged by God. But I am the one
who, through my *bechirah chofshis* (free will), determines
which path to take: "A," "B," or "C." If I (my body and soul)
choose path A, God will, in response, arrange a set of events,
circumstances, challenges, and people to be met, which I
will encounter upon my journey along my chosen path. If I
choose path B, then God will arrange a different set of
events, challenges, and people to be presented to me. I act
and choose; God reacts and guides. This is what we mean by

"having a relationship with God." This is what we mean by God's "guidance" or "providence." The events, circumstances, and hurdles presented to me by God are God's way of challenging me to serve Him and thus achieve my potential through the exercise of my free will.

להתעטף בציצת
My Morning Hug

Allow me to share with you a personal childhood recollection. As a child, I would wake up on a Monday morning after having spent a wonderful weekend with my family. We wouldn't only spend quality time together, we would spend real time together. On Sundays, we would go on family outings to parks, on country walks, or just play baseball in our backyard. I remember these warm family moments with special fondness to this day. I felt validated that my parents set aside their busy lives to spend valuable time with me and my younger brother and sister. I felt a bit insecure having to leave the cocoon of the family to go out into that big wide unknown, called Grade One. So on Monday mornings I would crawl into my parents' bed at 6:30 A.M., and snuggle up to Mom and Dad, and feel their warmth under the covers. I would try to hold onto one more moment of security before I ventured out into the world of arithmetic and bullies in the playground.

Now, I have a confession to make. Sometimes, even as an adult, with my own wife and children, as I prepare to leave the warmth and security of the family unit and venture out into the world of competition and free enterprise, I feel a pang of uneasiness and insecurity. I have to admit that I could do with and very much enjoy a warm, affirming hug just to give me a measure of inner strength with which to face the stormy tide outside. I guess old habits die hard.

And I do get that hug every morning. Besides the encouragement and *chizuk* that I get from my wife and children, I get the ultimate Hug — from Hashem. When I hold my tallis over my head and wrap my head and shoulders in the familiar black and white cloth, I feel a warm and life-affirming hug from God. I stand, with the four corners of the fringes gathered over my left shoulder, and I wait, sometimes five seconds, sometimes more. I feel the four corners of the world, the *"daled amos shel halachah"* ("the four cubits of Jewish law"), surround my inner being and infuse me with strength.

In the prayer immediately before donning the tallis, we say:

עֹטֶה אוֹר כַּשַּׂלְמָה.

He spreads out the light like a garment.

I clothe myself in the warmth of God's command — of God's embrace. After all, God's command is His way of relating to me. I relate to Him by trying to meet His requirements.

הֲרֵינִי מִתְעַטֵּף גּוּפִי בַּצִּיצִית, כֵּן תִּתְעַטֵּף נִשְׁמָתִי...בְּאוֹר הַצִּיצִית.

Behold, I wrap my body in these fringes; so, too, may my soul be enwrapped...in the spiritual light of the mitzvah of tzitzis.

May the light from my Source — Hashem — shine into my inner being and enwrap and enrapture my inner core.

Hug me with your warmth, O God, warm me with Your Presence as I yearn to be close to You.

תִּנָּצֵל נַפְשִׁי וְרוּחִי וְנִשְׁמָתִי וּתְפִלָּתִי מִן הַחִיצוֹנִים.

May my nefesh (my actions), and my ruach (my speech), and my neshamah (my thoughts), and my tefillah (my relationship with You, God), be rescued from external forces.

May I remain focused and aligned with Your will. May the inner strength I receive from my connection to You carry me through the ups and downs of this coming day. No matter what challenges You present to me, God, grant me the wisdom to realize that the ongoing connection of my *neshamah* to You can give me the strength to meet the challenges and adventures of the coming day. May I be granted the ability to draw upon this relationship (that I feel so warmly now with my tallis surrounding and strengthening me), and draw spiritual strength from You during the day, in my clinic, with my clients, in court, on my audit, on my delivery, in the midst of my contract negotiations.

If you walked into a tailor's shop to purchase a suit and found a beautiful suit with some threads still hanging on the edge of the pockets, would you buy that suit? Of course not. That suit has not been finished. So, too, it is with the fringes hanging from my tallis in the morning. When I put my tallis over my shoulder and look at the tzitzis dangling from the corners, I feel as if the fringes are speaking to me, challenging me. "Yisroel," the fringes are saying, "there is unfinished business to do in your world."[10] Hashem, through the tzitzis on the four corners of my garment, is speaking to me to "go for it," urging me to get on with my work. In Hebrew a garment is a *chaluk* — which has the same meaning as "*chelek,*" meaning "portion." When I put on my garment I am reminding myself to pursue my portion, my mission. Who says God doesn't speak to us anymore?

ברכות התורה
My Unique Contribution

There are only two *berachos* which are *d'oraisa* (Biblically required), namely *benching*[11] and *birchos haTorah* (the morning blessings of Torah study).[12] All the other blessings — *hanehenin* (e.g., food) and mitzvos (e.g., shofar) — are Rabbinically ordained. *Benching* is an acknowledgment that Hashem is the provider of our physical sustenance. The *birchos haTorah* are an acknowledgment that the Torah is the Source of our spiritual nourishment.

בָּרוּךְ אַתָּה ה' אֱלֹהֵינוּ מֶלֶךְ הָעוֹלָם, אֲשֶׁר קִדְּשָׁנוּ בְּמִצְוֹתָיו,
וְצִוָּנוּ לַעֲסוֹק בְּדִבְרֵי תוֹרָה.

Blessed are You, Hashem our God, King of the universe, Who has sanctified us with His commandments and commanded us to involve ourselves in the words of Torah.

The first blessing of *birchos haTorah* is formulated in the same terms as all *birchos hamitzvos,* namely "*asher kideshanu b'mitzvosav.*" The term "*kideshanu*" ("He has sanctified us") reminds me to focus on the sanctified *feeling* that I should experience when performing a mitzvah. The term *"kedushah"* (holiness) means an elevation of the physical to a higher, spiritual level. Saying these words should give me a sense of *simchah* in the realization that the study of Torah can cause me to raise the mundane to a spiritual plane. I can also do so by focusing on the spiritual sparks within everyday occurrences and by sanctifying them through following God's will.

The first of the three *berachos* that make up *birchos haTorah* is: *"...la'asok b'divrei Torah"* and is in reference to the study of the Torah *sheb'al peh* (Talmud).[13] The term *"la'asok"* means that we are entitled, in fact obligated, to involve ourselves in the process of the "give and take" of Torah analysis.

Even though Moshe Rabbeinu was taught all of the Torah by Hashem on Mount Sinai — including all Torah nuances that Jews in future generations would "discover" and expound[14] — it is the obligation of each of us to reveal those Torah *chiddushim* to the world. As we say at the end of the daily *Amidah* and during the Shabbos *Amidah*, *"V'sen chelkeinu b'Sorasecha"* — "Grant us our portion in your Torah." Each Jew has a God-given portion in Torah, that only he or she can bring to the world. This means that each of us has a unique potential and special contribution to make in revealing the Torah's depth and wisdom. If I expound or develop a new or novel thought in Torah, I can earn my portion in God's Torah. To attain my potential in this world, not only can I be *"mechadesh b'Torah"* — I am obligated to do so.

In the middle *berachah* of *birchos haTorah* we say:

וְהַעֲרֶב נָא...אֶת דִּבְרֵי תוֹרָתְךָ בְּפִינוּ.

Please sweeten...the words of Your Torah in our mouth...

The Maharsha[15] states that there is nothing more pleasing than the study of Torah, as it states, *"U'mesukim m'devash,"*[16] it is sweeter than honey. As we say in the song for Thursdays at the end of the prayer service: *"U'mitzur devash asbieka* — From the rock, honey will flow and satiate you."* This is an allusion to the honey of the Mishnah (Oral Law) which emanates from the Rock (the Written Law — the Five Books of Moses).

The Maharsha states that the term *"divrei Torascha"* refers to the study of the Mishnah. The *berachah* ends *"haMelamed Torah l'amo Yisrael* — the One Who teaches the Laws to His people Yisrael"* — which means that God is currently teaching us the Mishnah: the law emanating from the Torah.

The Talmud[17] states:

> And Rebbe Yehudah began his *drasha* (expounding of law) by giving honor to those who study Torah, and said: "Pay heed and listen, Israel you have become a nation...."[18] And Rebbe Yehudah said: "Was it really then that they became a nation? Weren't these words uttered by Moshe Rabbeinu at the end of their wanderings of forty years in the wilderness? It therefore teaches us that the Torah is beloved to those who study her wisdom everyday, as if it had been given to them this day from Mount Sinai!"

The fact that we achieved our status as a nation upon

our receiving the Torah gives us a great sense of belonging to the nation, if only we study the Torah. Moreover, just as the nation received its *kiyum* — its birth and its establishment — through the giving of the Torah, so too our *kiyum* — our existence — stems from our study of the Torah. Thus, the study of Torah everyday is akin to the opening of the flow of the Jewish nation's life force into our very being, thus reinvigorating us. In this way our *neshamah* is connected to its Source and is reenergized every day by plugging into the Source.

The Bach[19] states that the reason Hashem requires us to make a *berachah* prior to learning Torah is so that:

> Our *neshamah* shall be energized with the power, energy, and *kedushah* from the Source from whence the Torah devolves...so that the one who learns Torah shall be a chariot and palace for the Divine presence, such that the *Shechinah* shall actually establish its dwelling place within him, and this world will be enlightened by His Honor, and in this manner there shall be a link between the Heavenly Court and the Earthly Court, and God's Sanctuary shall be one...[and the learning of Torah] will cause the Divine presence to flow in the world.

Once we realize that we have the ability to bring God's presence into the world, we gain a sense of the crucial role that we play in the world. When we pray and learn, we do not transcend into the Heavenly spheres. Rather, we bring the Divine into our midst — into our very being.[20]

The final *berachah* of *birchos haTorah* states:

בָּרוּךְ אַתָּה...אֲשֶׁר בָּחַר בָּנוּ מִכָּל הָעַמִּים וְנָתַן לָנוּ אֶת תּוֹרָתוֹ.
בָּרוּךְ אַתָּה ה׳ נוֹתֵן הַתּוֹרָה.

Blessed are You... Who chose us from all nations and gave us His Torah. Blessed are You, Hashem, Giver of the Torah.

Hashem chose us from among all the nations of the world and decided to give us His Torah. "Not with you alone do I seal this covenant...but also with those who are not with us today."[21] Rabbeinu Bachya explains that just as the potential of the branches are contained in the parent tree, so future generations are contained in the parents who will give birth to them, and are bound by the parental covenant.

Thus, Hashem personally gave us His Torah when he gave it to the Jewish nation at Har Sinai. And Hashem personally chooses us every day to give us His Torah. Hence, the *berachah* ends in the present tense: *"Nosein haTorah"* — He Who gives the Torah anew every day.

Hashem wants me, as part of the Jewish nation, to be included in the transmission of His Torah. He wants to have a personal relationship with me. I can activate this relationship by speaking God's language — the study of Torah.

מזמור שיר חנוכת הבית לדוד
Highs and Lows

אֲרוֹמִמְךָ ה׳ כִּי דִלִּיתָנִי.

I will exalt You, Hashem, for You have drawn me up.

Life has its ups and downs. The opening psalm just prior to *Pesukei D'zimrah* reminds me to brace myself for the highs and lows of the forthcoming day, and also provides me with a method of how to deal with the day's challenges. The secret is in the word *dilisani*. The word *"dilisani"* has a double meaning. It comes from the same root as *"dli,"* a bucket. It goes down into the well but it also draws water out of the well. Life has its moments when the *dli* goes down into the well. We face crises, hurdles, and painful situations. It causes us to become *"dalim"* — *"poor"* and strained, frustrated and drained.

Yet a *dli* can be drawn up again, filled with water. While the rest of the world says, "What goes up must come down," the Jewish view is that "what goes down must come up." That is, it can come up if I do not despair and dig deep into the well to bring up the *dli*.

A person who has transgressed may find himself saddened. He may say: "I should have known better. I should have resisted the temptation. And I call myself a Jew?" This type of thinking may lead one to depression, a state of mind from which it is difficult to return — to do *teshuvah*. With the words *"Aromimcha Hashem ki dilisani* — I will exalt You, Hashem, for You have drawn me up,"* I categorically refute this faulty thinking process. True, I have made a mistake. I was less than scrupulous. But I must see my error in context. I am in the midst of a "process" of *teshuvah*. I may have slipped — but it is a slip on an upward slope. I have stumbled but I have not fallen to the base of the mountain. "Maintain your perspective," says David HaMelech. The bucket has gone down into the well; but I can also draw the bucket out of the well. It is a two-step process.

David HaMelech says: *"Shomer pesa'im Hashem dalosi*

v'li yehoshia — Hashem protects the foolish, I am down-trodden, but Hashem redeems me."[22] The Metzudas David explains the word *"dalosi"* as "when I was poor, He redeemed me in mitzvos."

The Talmud states: "Says Knesses Yisrael before Hashem: 'Master of the Universe, even though I am *dal* — poor in mitzvos — I belong to You and am worthy of your redemption.' "[23]

Think about it. "I belong to God." Say it again. One more time. I belong in God's world. He actually thinks about me. It is His will and desire that I be here in His world. Now that I am here, I must realize that God wants something from me. Not for His sake — He doesn't need anything. He wants me to give Him something — for my own sake. What does He want from me?

By virtue of my humanity and my weakness, I have a "built-in" opportunity to grow. The growth process is the most creative process a human being can undertake. If I err, I am a person "in process." I can rectify my mistake; I can do *teshuvah*, return to the right track. I can see my mistake as a potential to better myself. I can draw the *dli*, the bucket, out of the well of transgression, and behold it can be filled with fresh water — a new attitude, an advancement in my character and personality. All He wants from me is to draw the bucket out of the well and use the fresh water to renew myself as I serve Him.

ה׳ הֶעֱלִיתָ מִן שְׁאוֹל נַפְשִׁי.

Hashem, You have raised up my soul from the lower world.

One of the most painful emotional states is one of isolation and alienation even in the midst of a crowd. It is a feeling of "I don't belong here...in fact I don't belong anywhere." The Tikun Tefillah describes this as the "soul being in exile." It is a feeling of emotional angst like being disconnected from one's own "self." Am I really "alive"? The Eitz Chaim comments that through these words one pleads to Hashem to be redeemed or healed from this pain. If I say these words with *kavannah* I can actually feel Hashem lift me out of this anguish and redeem me. It is at this moment, in the midst of my pain, that I can actually feel a tangible connection and relationship with Hashem.

NOTES

1. Bereishis 29:35.
2. Rabbi Moshe Chaim Luzatto, *Derech Hashem.* Part 1, chapter 2 discusses the five parts of the soul. The first three, *nefesh, ruach,* and *neshamah,* are in this world. The root of the *neshamah,* made up of *chayah* and *yechidah,* is found in the higher spiritual world.
3. Yechiel Michel Tucazinsky, *Gesher HaChaim* (Jerusalem: Etz Chaim Publications, 1983), part 3, ch. 6, p. 126.
4. Bereishis 2:7.
5. *Sanhedrin* 91a.
6. Tucazinsky, p. 124.
7. Bereishis 24:4.
8. Ibid. 6:9.
9. The four spiritual dimensions upon which the world is based are:
   Asiyah — the physical world.
   Yetzirah — the forces of kindness and justice which are the foundations of nature and history.
   Beriah — the world of nature and history.
   Atzilus — the spiritual world from where souls emanate.
   See Rabbi Eliyahu Munk, *World of Prayer* (New York: Feldheim

Publishers, 1961), vol. 1, 11–13.

When we progress through *shacharis* we go through these four worlds as follows:

Asiyah — Birchos HaShachar
Yetzirah — Pesukei D'zimrah
Beriah — Birchos Krias Shema
Atzilus — Shemoneh Esrei.

10. Rabbi Uziel Milevsky, *z"l*, Ohr Somayach, Jerusalem, 1990.

11. Devarim 8:10 — "And you shall eat, and you shall be satisfied, and you shall bless Hashem your God for the goodly land that He gave you."

12. Ibid. 32:3 — "I will call on the Name of God; let us together utter praise of the greatness of Hashem." See *Berachos* 21a.

13. Rabbi Yaakov Emden, and *Beis Yosef*, *Orach Chaim*, end of ch. 47.

14. *Talmud Yerushalmi*, *Peah*, ch. 2, halachah 6.

15. *Berachos* 11b.

16. Tehillim 19:11.

17. *Berachos* 63b.

18. Devarim 27:9.

19. *Orach Chaim* 47.

20. Joseph B. Soloveitchik, *Halachic Mind* (Philadelphia: Jewish Publication Society of America, 1986), 94–5.

21. Devarim 29:13–14.

22. Tehillim 116:6.

23. *Pesachim* 118b.

Chapter 2

PESUKEI D'ZIMRAH —
SONGS OF PRAISE

ברוך שאמר והיה העולם
Empowerment

A young family with two boys, members of my for-
mer synagogue in London's West End, have two
pet tortoises in their garden, Lord and Lady
Brownstone. Bayswater in the West End is a beautiful resi-
dential area with large Victorian homes and walled back-
yards — or, as we say in England, "gardens." My children
and I were visiting this family one Sunday afternoon, and
my children were taken to the garden and became fascinated with the tortoises. The children were watching the
ten-inch creatures munch on some lettuce. The boys' father
remarked to me that if he were God, he would never have
even conceived of such a remarkable creature as the tortoise. The protective quilt-like shell, the slow sure-paced
legs, the hydraulic extending head, and those tiny almost
humanoid crunches of teeth as they munch through their
lettuce dinner, show the small reptile to be of an incredible,
intricate design. Only God could create such a complex

living thing. *"Mah rabu ma'asecha Hashem* — How wondrous are your works Hashem."[1]

If the animal kingdom is so wondrous and complex, then *kal v'chomer* the intricacies of the structure of the human being are that much more ingenious. Man can only stand in awe of the workings of his own body. Who was it that designed such teleological wonders as the human eye, with its one hundred million black and white receptors and seven million color receptors, the most complex camera ever devised? Who arranged the over one trillion circuits and connections in one human brain — more connections than exist in the entire world's communication system? Who devised the genetic DNA coding system, which carries more information in one double helix molecule than the most complex memory of any computer?[2] To the Designer of these systems, we offer praise.

Praise is defined as "acknowledging the greatness of another." *Pesukei D'Zimrah* (Songs of Praise) are introduced by the opening prayer *Baruch She'amar*: Blessed be the One who created the world with His speech. In this prayer, Hashem is called *"Yachid"* — He is unique, as Creator and Designer — and *"Chei Ha'olamim"* — the Sustainer of life and all worlds, Director of the stage that is the universe.

I have always wondered why it is considered so wondrous a thing that God created the tortoise, the human eye, photosynthesis, and the system which heals my son's bruises. After all, He can do anything. Indeed, from God's point of view, these creations are not so fantastic. He could have made them quicker or stronger. But from our vantage point they are incredible. *Pirkei Avos*[3] states that God did not need six days within which to create the world. He could have effected the entire creation in an instant. The only reason He chose to do it in six days is so that man could see and appreciate the progression and complexity of the systems of the universe. God did not create the world for Himself — but for man to recognize His Creator.

It was a wonderful *chesed* on the part of God to allow a finite created being like man to recognize and relate to Him — the Infinite Creator.

Bereishis begins with the words: "In the beginning God created the Heaven and the Earth." The purpose of the plan of Creation was for man to connect the Earth (the physical world) with the Heavens (the spiritual world) through *tefillah* — prayer.

The Torah states: "And all growing things were yet to grow..."[4] Rashi comments as follows:

> Why did it not yet rain? Because man was not in the world in order to work the land and was not yet placed in the world to recognize the bounty that is rain. When man arrived and realized that rains were necessary for the world, he prayed for rain and it fell and the trees and grass grew.

Rashi is teaching us that the entire creation was waiting for man to activate the process of nature's growth by praying to the Creator for rain. Adam was created alone so that each individual can identify with him. Thus I, as "man," have a crucial role to play in the universe. It doesn't work without me.

By recognizing God as the source of rain, man can "shake hands" with God every morning — by relating to Him through asking God to sustain and support him. The realization that my prayers activate the flow of rain, i.e., livelihood, is empowering. Recognizing that it is God Who is empowering me surely boosts my self-perception as a person who can effect significant change in the world.

I praise God to elevate myself to God's standards and values. The act of prayer itself can empower me to take responsibility for my actions and my character. It is certainly easier for me to develop my character if I focus on the standards, set out in the prayers, that God asks me to attain. Thus, prayer is much more than presenting God a "shopping list" of requests. It is an opportunity to relate to my Creator and to recharge my creative energies by "plugging in" to the Source of Creative Power Itself.

הודו לה׳
Making Every Day Meaningful

A friend of mine told me about a West End performance he attended in London's theater district. The old theaters give you a sense of medieval English culture, with their majestic painted ceilings and their exquisite royal boxes. The play my friend attended transported him back to the court of Richard III. He told me that after the play he went "backstage" to meet the lead actor. I was awe struck: "You actually know the lead actor?" I asked incredulously. I was amazed and a bit jealous. What an experience! To meet the creative genius of a talented Shakesperean actor is a real treat.

The Vilna Gaon explains the phrase *"hishallelu b'shem kadsho"* to mean that a person should recognize with joy the great gift he has been given in being allowed to praise His Creator — i.e., to go "backstage" and to connect with his own Source. To be able to praise the One Who designed the stage of the universe is a great privilege; to praise the Director Who has given me a lead role on the stage of my world is something to sing about. You actually know the world-famous Director? Sure, I have a close relationship with Him. I speak to Him every day.

At the end of this section we say: *"L'hodos l'shem kadshecha, l'hishtabeach bis'hilasecha* — to praise Your holy name, to become praised through praising You."* It is the ultimate *chesed* of Hashem that He uplifts me through the process of my prayers to Him. My praises of Hashem cannot possibly add to Him or His greatness. He is already "exalted beyond all exaltations"; He is already perfect. By asking me to praise Him, Hashem wants me to raise myself up to His standards. By praising Hashem's name, we mean His values and standards. I strive to reach those standards by living in accordance with halachah. Singing the same praises of Hashem every morning allows me to consistently visualize the goal of reaching Hashem's standards. This is the *"tefillah* process" — to connect with Hashem spiritually and to raise myself up to that spiritual standard by living those standards during the day.

When my *ratzon* (will) meets His *Ratzon* I create a sense of *deveikus* — a connection to God. If I appreciate this deeper dimension underlying my daily activities, even my superficial tasks can take on deeper meaning and significance. Everything I do can be seen as a step in the process of living in God's world and in becoming an *eved Hashem* — a servant of God. Buying milk at the corner store can take on the deeper significance that I am providing my family with the physical sustenance to be able to fulfill their spiritual obligations. Lining up at the bakery to get challos for Shabbos and preparing the Shabbos kugel and cholent can be seen as contributing to the Shabbos experience itself.

The physical world is the foundation and reflection of the spiritual world. My physical, menial tasks can be seen as a *hechsher mitzvah* — preparation for the performance of an actual mitzvah — thus injecting meaning into the process rather than only the mitzvah itself.

One of my teachers, Rabbi Efraim Oratz, tells the story of an old friend of his who delivered a package to his house on a Thursday evening. When he entered the house the magical smells of challah baking and brewing chicken soup filled the air, and he said: *"Shmeck fun Shabbos"* — the smell of Shabbos. He then confided that he was no longer Sabbath-observant, but the glorious smells reminded him of his childhood home on Thursday nights. That week, the man observed Shabbos for the first time in thirty years. The preparation for Shabbos is part of Shabbos. Since I heard this story I no longer complain about the long lines I have to endure to help my wife with the pre-Shabbos purchases.

מזמור לתודה
Happiness through Suffering

The Talmud tells us that the *korban sodah* (the thanksgiving offering), which was brought by an individual in the Temple in gratitude for a personal miracle that had happened, is going to be the only sacrifice still offered after the coming of Mashiach. The reason is that "giving thanks" is the foundation of my relationship with God. When I realize I have received the gift of being privileged to play a role in God's world — my daily existence takes on new meaning. In this psalm I don't only thank Hashem for the extraordinary miracles that He has performed; I say thank you to God for the miracle of life itself.[5]

Making a *berachah* on a fruit or other food is not so much for God as it is for me. When I realize that God is personally giving me a gift of this fruit — because He wants to display His *chesed* towards me — then I energize my relationship with Him. He has given, and is always ready, willing, and able to give. Hashem holds out His hand and I shake His hand in acknowledgment of His gift by making a *berachah*. It is man who brings the produce full circle to its Source with his thanksgiving offering. Man observes the wonder of this world and elevates the physical world, i.e., an apple, by recognizing God as its Source. Thus, blessings on food in particular, and prayer in general, keep us in a constant state of amazement of the world by causing us to connect even the mundane physical world with its spiritual Source.

Where does an apple come from? A tree. Where does the tree come from? A seed in an apple. Where did that apple come from? A previous tree. Where did that tree come from? A seed from a previous apple. The biological chain goes back to the very first tree. Had there been a break in the chain of tree, apple, seed...anywhere in history, I would not be enjoying this apple. All future apples were "in God's mind" at the creation of the first apple in the Garden of Eden. When I make a *berachah* over an apple, I pause for a moment and am awestruck by the notion that God directed the entire course of nature and history in order to give me — yes me — this apple. God had me in mind when He created the first tree. When I make a *berachah* I am saying, "Thanks for the chain of apples, God. Thanks for thinking of me."[6]

In this psalm we say, *"Ivdu es Hashem b'simchah —*

Serve Hashem with joy." Every second of our lives can be infused with energy and meaning if we relate everything that happens in our lives to God. When things go well — I thank God. When things are tough — I thank God for thinking that I am worth prodding or guiding to higher levels of achievement through this crisis or challenge. This is real *simchah*: an inner tranquility, an inner peace, which is a by-product of this type of meaningful relationship with God.

Now, sometimes I am not in the mood to serve God *b'simchah*. I may not be feeling well, my kids may be acting up, I may be under pressure at work, and I may not have been able to get to my weekly *shiur* in two months. In these circumstances how can I serve Hashem with inner tranquility? On what basis can God command me to serve Him "in joy" if the ordeals He has presented me with bring me to a state of travail and depression?

The commentaries teach us that serving Hashem *b'simchah* does not mean that I should be smiling and laughing in the face of adversity. The goal is to face and to go through the ordeal or trial knowing that this is precisely what God wants me to be working through at the present moment. Through the difficult issue with which He is confronting me, he is teaching me that my *neshamah* needs to be going through this difficulty right now so that I can grow and develop my *middos*, and through this process come closer to achieving my potential, i.e., the development of my personality. This particular trial is the purpose for my being in the world right now. The only way I can attain true inner tranquility and peace is by facing and working through this issue. And this very realization should produce an inner calm despite the outer pain, frustration, and anxiety.

Of course the test I am currently facing itself challenges my faith in God. That, in fact, is the *nisayon* — to be challenged in my faith, to grapple with my pain and doubts, to learn something from the process and thereby pass the test by maintaining my faith. True *simchah* can only be attained by ascending from one level of character development to the next. The process of changing from one mind-set or set of values, and moving on to the next mind-set or level is what we mean by "growth." The growth or development process is itself the source of true *simchah* — joy.

When people face and grapple with their problems, the growth they achieve through the pain and suffering is a refinement of character which is spiritual — and thereby true *simchah*. In every situation, in the midst of the ordeal that I am facing, I have an opportunity to mentally visualize what type of growth Hashem is seeking from me. The realization that Hashem Himself has assigned this challenge out of His desire for my spiritual growth creates a *deveikus* with God that produces *simchah*. It is through facing this challenge that I will make my personal contribution to the world.[7] For example, Yaakov Avinu went through the ordeal of overcoming his own hesitations and deferring to his mother's *ruach hakodesh* — Divine direction — by deceiving his father Yitzchak and receiving the blessing of the firstborn. And as a result of that ordeal the world was given the eternal principle: "*Hakol kol Yaakov v'hayadayim yedei Esav* — the voice is the voice of Yaakov, the hands are the hands of Esav." This principle teaches the world that the voice, the power of the "word," is more powerful than the hand, or sword.[8] This has been the message of the Jew to the world. It only came about through Yaakov facing his ordeal and making his contribution despite his misgivings and personal quandry.

Rashi tells us that when Yaakov fled from Esav and lived with the immoral Lavan for twenty years, he was still able to keep the Torah's 613 commandments despite the negative influences of his environment.[9] It was an ordeal to be faced with the tricks and deceit of Lavan. But it was Yaakov's adherence to Torah values in the face of Lavan's immorality which was Yaakov's eternal contribution to the world. If he could do it, there is precedent for me to follow.

Rashi also quotes the midrash that when Yaakov was escaping from Esav after Esav threatened to kill him, Yaakov was confronted by Elifaz, Esav's son, who threatened his life.[10] Yaakov gave up his possessions and enshrined forever the sanctity of life over materialism, in the Torah for all to see. In the first recorded mugging in history, Elifaz effectively said: "Your money or your life." Yaakov said: "Take my money. Give me my life." He achieved this through being faced with the threat of death by his nephew.

It is through Yaakov's being away from his parents for twenty-two years in the house of Lavan that we learn the principle of "middah k'neged middah." He was punished for his failure to honor his parents for those twenty-two years by having his own son Yosef removed from him during the twenty-two years that Yosef spent in Egypt. Through this torturous test the world learns the principle of the balance of justice in the world. Yaakov's ordeal gave rise to this principle.

It is through the ordeal of being pressed by the seductive advances of the wife of Potifar that Yosef obtains the title "Yosef HaTzadik." He resisted the temptation and went to prison falsely accused but having maintained the principles of morality. He could only have taught us this eternal lesson had he gone through the ordeal.

The *Beis HaMikdash* in Jerusalem came about as the result of David HaMelech's ordeal. David HaMelech sinned by counting the people directly in a census. A plague ensued and seventy thousand people died. David HaMelech was instructed to build an altar at the threshing floor of Aravnah the Yevusi (Jebusite) and to pray for the atonement of his sin and for his people there.[11] That threshing floor became the place upon which the *Beis HaMikdash* was later built.

My natural reaction to an ordeal, pain, and suffering may be a feeling of anger or frustration. These are normal external reactions to the physical and emotional strain. But these feelings must remain external reactions to the ordeal. The anger and frustration must never be allowed to penetrate so deeply into my psyche that they bring me to despair or depression. The successful passage through the process of the trial will teach me and others an important lesson — which is the purpose of my ordeal.

In a sense, I must step back from my predicament while it is happening and look at myself from God's perspective. Going through this ordeal with a consciousness that this is God's will and that working through it is actually my purpose in life at this particular moment — will give me strength to persevere. The perseverance and growth will create a sense of inner *simchah* in the midst of the external sadness. The growth in character that results from weathering the process of the test will bring me to a new level of inner peace.

When a woman goes through the pain of labor and childbirth, it is the labor itself which urges the baby along the birth canal. Therefore, the physical travail and pain of the process of childbirth are necessary to actually produce life. It is the pain of the ordeal which urges us to give birth to a new level of "self."

When Yosef tested his brothers when they came down to Egypt to seek food, he put them through a painful ordeal. Through their ordeal, Yosef maneuvered his brothers into position to do *teshuvah* for having sold him into slavery.

Yosef accused his brothers of being spies; he held Shimon captive while they returned to bring Binyamin to Egypt. They were shocked to find money in their sacks on the way back to Canaan, and were falsely accused of theft. They returned now only to have Binyamin's sack found to contain the cup of the king. They were told to leave Binyamin as a servant of Yosef. What was going through their minds as they went through these trials?

The Rambam in *Hilchos Teshuvah* sets out the three-step *teshuvah* process, as follows:

1. *Charatah* — remorse over the transgression;

2. *Vidui* — verbal confession;

3. *Kabalah le'asid* — resolve never to repeat the transgression.[12]

When Yosef took Shimon from his brothers, they were reliving their transgression: they had taken Yosef from their own midst and dragged him into the pit. The brothers exhibited remorse for their past actions when they said: "We are guilty on account of our brother when he pleaded to us and we did not hear his pleas; therefore this evil comes upon us."[13] They thus completed Step One of the *teshuvah* process by showing remorse.

They then fulfilled Step Two of the *teshuvah* process

when the cup of the king was found in the sack of Binyamin, and Yehudah, speaking for his brothers, confessed: "What can we say to our master, what can we utter, how can we justify? The Lord has found the transgression of your servants."[14]

Finally, when they were placed in precisely the position to repeat their transgression by being given the option of abandoning Binyamin in Egypt and returning to Israel, Yehudah, who originally suggested the sale of Yosef,[15] said: "And now let me be a slave to my master instead of the lad, and let the lad go up with his brothers."

It is with this action that the brothers achieved *teshuvah gemurah*. The pain of the ordeal itself created a transformation of the brothers from "sin" to "repentance" and thus achieved the forgiveness of God. When they realized that the ordeal Yosef put them through itself served to rectify their flawed character, they then understood that the ordeal was for their ultimate benefit. In retrospect, they would never have forgone their ordeal, because through it they achieved repentance and a closer relationship with God.

Yosef, who was the organizer of their torturous ordeal, was also the source of their redemption when he revealed himself to them with the words: *"Ani Yosef, ha'od avi chai?* — I am Yosef, is my father still alive?"*

The one who caused their ordeal was also their redeemer. He was the one who put them through the ordeal, and he ended the process by revealing himself to them. The message is clear. The ordeal itself, if it is successfully met, *is* the redemption. Even though I might not know why I am going through a particular difficulty, the realization that the process itself is necessary to attain a required development of my character or personality, gives me the strength to withstand the test. What looked like pain is actually the medium which led to my change in character, which in turn creates within me *simchah* — the sweetness of achievement, growth, and, thus, inner peace. The transition from one level of personality to the next gives rise to real inner joy. The external sadness produced by the ordeal remains superficial to my internal realization of my "service of God *b'simchah*" — when I extract spiritual growth from my ordeal.[16]

יהי כבוד
Seize the Day

The inspiring Latin maxim "carpe deim — seize the day" expresses man's longing to get the most out of life. While Judaism clearly teaches a different path to achieving that goal than does neo-Platonic philosophy, we too strive to "capture the moment." It is an elusive task indeed.

The present moment is the millisecond when the future meets the past. When I was growing up, I was always fascinated by the truism: "Today will be yesterday, tomorrow." Can we actually seize or freeze the "today" present moment and capture its meaning? I fear not. As soon as I reach out to savor a particularly wonderful moment, i.e., a birthday, a warm heart-to-heart talk, the success of meeting a deadline, the moment itself slips into the past. It is not possible for human beings to actually "live in the present moment" because the moment is dynamic and won't stand still. Am I then destined to merely anticipate the future and to savor the memories of the past without ever actually having lived in the present?

This psalm, *Yehi Ch'vod*, answers that it is possible to experience the present.

"*Hashem Melech, Hashem Malach, Hashem Yimloch, l'olam va'ed* — God is King, God was King, God will be King forever." This compilation of three verses in Tehillim and Torah[17] indicates that God, Who is beyond time, can and does live in the past, present, and future simultaneously. He Who created time, must transcend time. The only way for a human being to transcend time, or even capture or seize a given moment in time, as if to make time stand still, is to enter into a relationship with God Who transcends time.[18]

How does one achieve or actualize this relationship with God? There are 613 avenues or pathways to relate to God: they are the "*taryag* mitzvos."[19] Each commandment provides an opportunity to "meet" God. The root word of "mitzvah" is "*tzeves*" — which means to connect or to bind. When I fulfill the mitzvos I connect with God. If I follow God's will through the Torah then I am achieving "*deveikus*" or embrace of God. The moment of connection with Timeless God, in the midst of performing a mitzvah, is the moment I can "capture" by seizing its majesty. When I live in this mitzvah connection, I am actually living in the present. I have captured the moment. It becomes eternalized. I create a spiritual eternity even in the midst of this physical world.

Through prayer, I can express my appreciation for the gift of living in connection with God. The *Pesukei D'Zimrah* allow me to contemplate God as the Creator and as the God of History. I stand in awe of God's interaction with the world — His wondrous world of nature and His guiding hand through history. Then I enter into a private, heart-to-heart conversation with God when I embrace Him

during the *Amidah*. This is the moment my *ratzon* can meet
His *Ratzon*. In the moments of praise (*Pesukei D'Zimrah*)
and in private conversation (*Amidah*), I can achieve an intimate, warm embrace with God. This, and the performance
of a mitzvah, is the way to capture the present — by embracing the only One who actually Lives in the present.

אשרי
Actualizing My Potential

The Talmud assures us that: "Whoever recites
Tehillah L'David (*Ashrei*) three times a day [twice in
shacharis and once in *minchah*] is assuredly worthy
of a share in the World to Come."[20]

The Talmud explains that the reason for such a reward is
that *Ashrei* is unique in Tehillim in that it contains two special
elements: 1) an alphabetical acrostic, and 2) the verse:
"Poseach es yadecha u'masbea l'chol chai ratzon — You open
up Your hand and satisfy the needs of every living thing."

The Maharasha explains that the alphabetical acrostic,
which contains wondrous praises of God, teaches us that we
can serve God with every letter of the *alef-beis*, i.e., with every bit of our energy and at every moment. We can use every
one of the talents that God has given us, and every weakness
that He challenges us with, to achieve our purpose in life
and thereby truly praise God.

The second special element of *Ashrei* is the concept of
hashgachah pratis (Divine Providence), which is embodied in the
verse *"Poseach es yadecha"* — He prepares the food and sustenance of every living thing. It is by virtue of affirming these two
principles that a person who says *Ashrei* with proper *kavanah* is
worthy of earning his or her place in the World to Come.

Etz Yosef tell us that the verse previous to *"Poseach es yadecha,"* which reads: *"Einei chol eilecha yisabeiru v'Atah nosein lahem es ochlam b'ito* — The eyes of all look expectantly to You and You give them their food at its proper time,"* is actually an acknowledgment that God provides for each individual's physical sustenance, shelter, clothing, possessions, and all his particular needs. If so, asks the Maharasha, [21] what does *"Poseach es yadecha"* come to add? The Maharasha answers that the verse *"Poseach es yadecha"* does not say that God satisfies us with food. Rather it says: *"U'masbea l'chol chai ratzon"* — *ratzon* (will) instead of *mazon* (food).

Thus the Maharasha answers that I am not praising Hashem for physical sustenance, because that is covered by the previous verse. Here, I am praising Hashem for satisfying me with spiritual nourishment, i.e., allowing me to have and express my inner will. My free will is given to me so that ultimately I will give it up to serve Hashem.[22] When I learn God's will, which means when I learn what God wants from the world in general and for me in particular, and live in accordance with His will, then my *neshamah* receives spiritual nourishment. This does not mean that God will satisfy or grant my every request. Rather, the gift of free will is, in and of itself, the satisfaction and nourishment that my soul craves. To be aware of my ability to serve God through the exercise of my free will is an energizing realization. It can be a spiritual boost to my inner self to realize that God has confidence in me that I can serve Him, achieve my potential, and make a valuable contribution to society. God believes that I am mature enough to make my own choices and that I can choose wisely. God Himself believes in me. What better support can I ask for?

By making my will match God's will through studying and applying the Torah to my life, I earn the reward of my portion in the World to Come. Now, how do we merit the World to Come? The World to Come is created by our growth in character in this world. The development of my character and values is itself the creation of my portion for eternity. I will only live in the next world by virtue of that spiritual reality that I created in this world by facing the challenges of life and growing as a better, kinder, more giving person. The Torah gives me the general framework of how to respond to the challenges and issues in life in a manner that will cause my soul to develop to its potential. If, for example, I am an angry person, one of my challenges in life is to temper my anger and channel that passion into positive, creative energy. The Talmud teaches us that anger is a negative character trait. It urges us to change and to grow. When I grow in character I create a spiritual "world." I will live in that world in the World to Come.[23]

Soon after my family and I moved to England in 1991, my wife gave birth to our third child — on Yom Kippur, no less. It was my first Yom Kippur in the shul and she gave birth at 6 A.M. on Yom Kippur morning. I got a bit lost walking to shul from the Hammersmith Hospital — the one-hour walk took me two and a half hours. This scenario was to characterize our hectic first months in London. A few weeks later, I came home after a day of teaching and meetings, not having slept the night before, due to our new daughter's feeds. I came home, the house was a mess, diapers were everywhere, dishes all over the kitchen, my wife feeding the baby. As I was about to comment on the state of the house and ask about dinner, I caught myself and said to Julie:

"Looks like you've had a tough day. I'm sorry I haven't been here for you. What can I do to help you?" I worked on myself by refraining from complaining and turned a difficult situation into one of sensitivity. I like to think that I created a small measure of spiritual growth which, God willing, I will live in, in the World to Come.

In *Ashrei*, we praise Hashem with every letter of the *alef-beis*. We praise Hashem *"bechol yom"* — every day, every second. We teach God's will to the next generation — *"dor l'dor."* We emulate God by acting kindly and mercifully to others — and thereby show that He is *"Chanun v'Rachum,"* kind and merciful. We hold back our anger by emulating God's being *"Erech Apayim,"* long suffering. We know that everything Hashem sends our way affords us an opportunity to grow and to fulfill our potential, and we thus declare: *"Tov Hashem la'kol* — God is good to all."

Thus, we take every letter of our daily *"alef-beis,"* i.e., our daily experience in this world, and we earn our place in the World to Come. How? By conducting our journey through this world in accordance with the *"Masbea l'chol chai ratzon"* — the *ratzon* of Hashem, as outlined and taught to us in the Torah. God is close to us — *"Karov Hashem l'chol kor'av"* — and is ready to be involved in our lives. When we find the sanctity in everyday living, by injecting *kedushah* into the *alef-beis* — the details of our day to day lives — then we succeed in growing and building our spiritual place in the World to Come.

Each of us can find our names in the Torah. The Hebrew word for "name" is *"shem."* The two Hebrew letters of the word *"shem,"* *shin* and *mem*, make up the two middle letters of the word *"neshamah."* I can gain an insight into the essence of my *neshamah* if I look at my Hebrew name. If my name is Yisroel, it can be seen as a quasi-description of my soul's essence and task in this world. I, like Yaakov, must "strive with Godly issues and with man" and bring praise of God to the world. If I succeed in bringing honor to Hashem, then I will have become worthy of the name Yisroel. If my name is Avraham or Sarah, it is possible that one of my tasks is to exhibit *chesed* toward my family and community, as the *middah* or attribute of Avraham and Sarah was *chesed*. Sarah was a "princess of dignity": the word "*sar*" means nobleman or prince.

I can also learn more about my spiritual self by referring to the verse in *Tanach* that begins with the first letter of my Hebrew name and ends with the last letter of my name. These verses can be found in most *siddurim* (including Artscroll). The meaning and commentaries on this verse often come very close to describing one's personality.

By understanding the meaning of my Hebrew name, or gaining insight into the character of the Biblical personality after whom I am named, I can find a hint about my soul's inclination and purpose. In this way I can learn more about myself, what I need to work on, and how I can develop my spiritual self so that I can live in that eternal "self" in the World to Come.

God does not want me to experience the "bread of shame" by being granted my reward in the Next World without earning it. So he challenges me to meet the trials and ordeals of life, and gives me the Torah with which to guide me as I meet the challenges that He unfolds before me.

God has incredible confidence in me! I can achieve greatness, scholarship, good character attributes, and achieve my potential if I rely on God's standards. *"She'El Yaakov b'ezri* — the God of Yaakov will help me" to actualize my personal *yichus* (stature). It is not sufficient for me to rely on the fact that I am a descendant of great people. I must realize that one day I am going to be an ancestor of great people. It is mind-blowing to realize that my grandchildren will look back to me as their "Zaidy." This means that I have the ability to shape the foundations of future generations. I suppose this is an answer to the question posed by a famous contemporary Jewish song: Who will be the Zaidys of our children — if not me?[24]

There was a popular film in the 1980s called *Back to the Future* where the star was transported back into his own past in a time machine. While in the "past" he changed one of his original actions, and the result was that when he got "back to the future," his present life, his whole destiny, had changed by virtue of that one past modification. If only I could imagine my "present" as a moment of opportunity to affect my future destiny, then one small change for the better, one extra ounce of effort to do that which I always wanted to do but never got around to doing — could change my life and the lives of future generations.

הללוי-ה הללי נפשי
Personal Merit

אַל תִּבְטְחוּ בִנְדִיבִים.

O*Do not place your trust in noblemen.*
ur Sages teach us that we should not put our trust in princes or aristocrats. We should not even rely

on our sainted ancestors, Avraham, Yitzchak, and Yaakov, for deliverance. Doesn't the concept of *zechus avos*, "merit of our forefathers," bode well for me? Can't I rely on their greatness? After all, each of us is proud of the fact that somewhere in our family *yichus* there is a sainted rabbi, teacher, author, or communal leader. I often hear someone say: I may not be observant but my great grandfather was a great scholar. Is David HaMelech telling me to stop being proud of my lineage? No. He is merely telling me that it is not enough to rely on my family background. He is urging me to get on with my personal merit — known as *yichus atzmis*. I can't rely on the past glories of my family's contributions to the Jewish people. David HaMelech wants me to actualize my personal potential for greatness.

הללוי-ה כי טוב
Loneliness vs. Being Alone

Whenever I experience family, financial, or career pressures overwhelming me, I am directed by David HaMelech to place my sincere faith in Hashem that He is: *"Harofei lishvurei lev u'mechabeish l'atzvosam"* — He is the healer of the broken hearted and also binds up their wounds.

The act of placing my trust in Hashem, and of asking Hashem to share in and to relieve my pain and suffering, is the process which itself helps in the healing of my wounds.

Some mornings I have such a feeling of low self-esteem and negative self-worth that I hardly feel like getting out of bed. How do I initiate this process of asking Hashem to heal my pain when I feel so overwhelmed and weak that I hardly have the strength to lift up my burdens and carry them to God's doorstep?

It is at this moment that the morning service continues:

מוֹנֶה מִסְפָּר לַכּוֹכָבִים, לְכֻלָּם שֵׁמוֹת יִקְרָא.

He fixes the numbers of the stars; He calls all of them by name.

The Jewish people are compared to stars.[25] Each of us has a bright light within us which can shine if only we realize the special talents that we possess. When I contemplate my unique combination of strengths and weaknesses, I realize that I am alone in the world. It is my uniqueness which makes me alone. This is not the same as being lonely. It is alright to feel alone within the world. The only way I can be a star and to make my special contribution in the night sky is to stand alone.[26]

According to Rabbi Joseph B. Soloveitchik, being alone should not elicit feelings of loneliness. Rather, it should instill in me a sense of *simchah* in that I have a God-given, unique role to play in God's world, which only I can fulfill. Thus, the positive aspect of being "alone in the world" is that I am unique in the world. Through growing through my ordeals and crises, I become what only I can become.

I will make the unique contribution that my name represents. God calls all of His stars "by name" — he has a purpose for each person and gives each of us a special role to play as unique to the spiritual world as our DNA is unique to the physical world. God has "hand picked" a plan for me. My star, my name, is known to God. I am part of His plan. He wants me to make my contribution. But I can't do it by sleeping away the mornings in a depressive, listless state.

גָּדוֹל אֲדוֹנֵינוּ וְרַב כֹּחַ, לִתְבוּנָתוֹ אֵין מִסְפָּר. מְעוֹדֵד עֲנָוִים ה'.

Great is our Master and abundant in power; His understanding is beyond reckoning. Hashem causes the humble to stand firm.

I can draw strength from placing my trust in God, by recharging my batteries with energy from the Generator — God. But I do have to get out of bed and insert the plug into the socket. God can make the humble stand firm. He will not make the depressed, self-pitying person stand firm unless he or she is willing to make an effort. It is humbling to contemplate being part of God's cosmic plan. But it is also inspiring and empowering to realize that God expects me to make my humble contribution to that cosmic plan.

If He has a plan for me then why does He make things so difficult for me?

God directs, controls, and chooses each circumstance presented to every individual — and each circumstance is necessary for that person's personal growth. Each of us is called upon to give the best possible response that he is capable of giving. This is all that God expects of us. It does not mean, however, that I will necessarily be able to overcome this particular crisis or challenge or see the problem through to a happy resolution. The "best possible response" may mean that I am able to withstand the difficulty, live with the condition or situation, and come to terms with my inability to solve the problem. If, however, I am unable to achieve even this, then it is clear that this was not a test; rather, it was something I had to go through which will help my spiritual growth in a different way.

According to Rabbi Eliyahu Dessler,[27] there are two types of "mazal" or "destiny." There is a *mazal tachton* — a this-world destiny which can be changed through prayer, personal growth, and kind deeds, which I activate through the exercise of my free will. A crisis sent to me under the rubric of *mazal tachton* is a test to be solved or withstood and seen to a successful conclusion. However, a challenge sent to me from *mazal elyon* — beyond-this-world destiny — is not meant to be solved but endured. Thus, some difficulties are not tests for me to solve. They are sent to me because this is what my soul must go through in order to achieve its *tikun* — "rectification" or ultimate destiny.

Rabbi Moshe Chaim Luzatto,[28] states that God's *Chochmah HaElyon* (Highest Wisdom) determines each person's appropriate challenge in order to attain *shleimus*, perfection. If I know that I am on a path toward "perfection," this will, in and of itself, give me a sense of inner tranquility. Even though I have not yet "made it" I am "in process" — and being in the midst of the search for spirituality and perfection is the essence of serving God.

Some people are challenged with poverty; some live through war time; some are challenged with a disability or illness... all in order for his or her soul to fulfill itself in service of Hashem. These are not punishments but are necessary for my complete service of Hashem, to push me to the level of a true *eved Hashem* — servant of God. Sometimes a person must endure suffering and pain. That person's challenge is to know that while he or she can do nothing to change the situation, he or she must maintain faith in God.

Surely this is a very high level of service of God. Not everyone can achieve this. It does, however, help me answer the question: "Why is God doing this to me?" The answer is "because He loves me and wants me to perfect myself by living with and through this problem." This realization gives me comfort in that it does not mean that God is angry with me or is rejecting me. He has His reasons and I must try to give myself over to Him. I can thus stand in prayer before God and say, "Cast upon Hashem your burden and He will sustain you."[29] I accept this burden, Hashem, now please share it with me. In this fashion, even in the midst of my pain I can feel close to God.

The Torah states: *"U'Moshe nigash el ha'arafel asher sham HaElokim* — And Moshe drew near to the thick cloud where God was."[30] According to Nesivos Shalom, this means that Moshe knew then, even in the midst of the "thick cloud," where I find myself surrounded by darkness and difficulty, there, God can be found.

There is a story told of a man who wanted to understand why people suffer. He was told to find a certain elderly man who lived at the outskirts of a faraway town — and he would reveal to him the meaning of suffering. He finally found the old man, who was living in abject poverty, whose body was covered in disease, and who could barely see.

"I am told that you can tell me the meaning of suffering," said the young man.

"I don't know why you have come to me," said the old man. "What is suffering? I am a servant of Hashem. Thank God for every day."

The Jewish approach to suffering is that one second of life is immeasurably holy and infinitely wonderful, notwithstanding the suffering one might be going through. Western values suggest that the purpose of life is to achieve "happiness." Thus people think that experiencing pain negates the purpose of life. Judaism teaches that the purpose of life is to live a meaningful life in accordance with Hashem's will. The process of achieving *sheleimus* sometimes entails crises and challenges which I must endure in order to be a true servant of Hashem. The by-product of living such a meaningful life is true *simchah*, inner fulfillment, and inner peace.

הללוי-ה, הללו את ה׳
Personal Growth

Many people go through personal identity crises which cause them to seek to "find themselves" in the midst of a complex world. This psalm describes the ever increasing levels of complexity of the world and gives me a formula for identifying my place within it. In this psalm I can "find myself" by allowing the words to direct my attention to focus on my unique position in the universe, as follows:

Level 1:

אֵשׁ וּבָרָד, שֶׁלֶג וְקִיטוֹר...הֶהָרִים וְכָל גְּבָעוֹת...

Fire and hail, snow and vapor...the mountains and all the hills....

These are the lowest level of creation known as *domem*, inanimate creations, which *"oseh dvaro"* — serve God by fulfilling their role as the basic elements of Creation. They serve as the bottom line or bedrock of the universe.

Level 2:

עֵץ פְּרִי וְכָל אֲרָזִים...

Fruit trees and cedars...

The second level in the hierarchy of Creation is known as *tzameach* — that which grows, i.e., the plant kingdom. This level is distinguished from the previous inanimate stage in that it has a basic level of life: growth.

Level 3:

הַחַיָּה וְכָל בְּהֵמָה, רֶמֶשׂ וְצִפּוֹר כָּנָף.

Wild beasts and all animals, creeping things, and winged fowl.

The third link in the chain is that which is *chai* — alive with an animated, dynamic physical soul known as *nefesh habehamis*, the animal soul. The animal kingdom, which reacts not by reason but by instinct, shares this crude animal soul with man in his most basic form.

Level 4:

מַלְכֵי אֶרֶץ וְכָל לְאֻמִּים, שָׂרִים וְכָל שֹׁפְטֵי אָרֶץ. בַּחוּרִים וְגַם בְּתוּלוֹת, זְקֵנִים עִם נְעָרִים.

Earthly kings and all peoples, ministers and all earthly judges. Young men and also maidens, elders together with lads.

The crown of God's creation is not known as "man" but as *"medaber"* — the one who speaks. Once I realize that I, as a *medaber*, am the most complex creature in the universe, I immediately gain a sense of intrinsic worth by recognizing my role in God's hierarchy. The lower forms, i.e. inanimate, plant, and animal life, are to be utilized by me to assist me in fulfilling my role in creation. But what is that role?

The next verse in this psalm provides the answer:

יְהַלְלוּ אֶת שֵׁם ה׳.

Praise God's Name.

The goal and purpose of life is to praise God's name, to increase *kavod Shamayim* — the honor of God in the world — and thereby come closer to Him. I praise God by introducing *kedushah* to the world through striving to adhere to God's standards of ethical and moral conduct as expressed in the Torah. I can bring *kedushah* to the world by acting in accordance with Hashem's will in the spheres *bein adam l'Makom* and *bein adam l'chaveiro* — between man and God, and between man and his fellowman.

Striving to refine my character is itself service of God. I can develop my "*middos*" — character — by emulating God's attributes. The Talmud tells us: "Since God is merciful so, too, shall you act mercifully."[31] By praising God's attributes I remind myself of the standards of behavior I should try to attain. Through this process I can be among those referred to at the conclusion of this psalm:

לִבְנֵי יִשְׂרָאֵל עַם קְרֹבוֹ, הַלְלוּיָהּ.

For the children of Israel, the people near to Him, Praise God.

If I come near to God by incorporating His will into my life, then my life in and of itself will be a praise of Hashem. If

I step closer to God, He will step closer to me. When each individual strives to achieve his potential, then the nation of Israel as a whole is strengthened.

הללוי-ה, שירו לה׳ שיר חדש
Because You Are Mine

In this psalm we are urged by David HaMelech: "Sing to God a new song; sing His praise in the assembly of the pious." The true praise of God is a song where each individual adds his unique voice to the community symphony. Thus the song sung by the Israelites after they crossed the Sea was the ultimate praise of God since it was acclaimed publicly, as King Solomon teaches us: *"B'rov am hadras Melech — With a greater multitude I praise the King."*[32]

Not only do I have a personal relationship with God but I can also relate to Him as a member of the nation of Israel. I can draw strength in the realization that I am a personal shareholder in the great corporate structure of the Jewish people — the assembly of Israel.

כִּי רוֹצֶה ה׳ בְּעַמּוֹ.

Because Hashem desires His people.

It is arguably the most affirming, warm feeling of security to be loved and appreciated. When I tell my child I love her, I go on to ask her: "Do you know why I love you?" She says, "Why?" "Because you are mine," I assure her, as I give her a warm hug.

That expression of belonging to me, coupled with my daughter nestled in my arms, gives her a feeling of acceptance and security. When God says He "desires" us, He is saying: "I love you, My people, because you are Mine." God wants a relationship with His people. He wants us to attend regular shareholders' meetings (minyan) as well as corporate board meetings (Torah study *shiurim*).

Isn't it a wonderful feeling when the Chairman of the Board knows my name, smiles at me, and says: "Have a nice day." That's what God says to me as an individual when He returns my soul to me in the morning. That is what He is saying to me when He asks me to attend minyan to make up the quorum of shareholders. That is what He is saying to me through the words of the Torah when I sit down to study His Torah. Feeling wanted makes me want to sing a *shir chadash* — a new song.

Not only am I expressing a new song, I feel *hischadshus* — renewed by Hashem's love, and that in and of itself is my song to Him. For harmony to be achieved in the choir, each voice must sing its special melody. To sing, out of the knowledge that God accepts me and desires to hear my song — gives me personal strength and encouragement.

הללוי-ה הללו קל בקדשו
Getting in Touch with My Soul

Some mornings everything seems to go right. I wake up one second before the alarm. I feel rested. (This might happen only once a year — but it does happen.) My coffee is just right, my spouse is humming as I walk out the door. The bus arrives fifteen seconds after I get to the bus stop or I catch every green light on the way into the office. My work projects are going smoothly. The kids are well. In short, I'm "flying." I am "on" — connected and energized. Why? My body and soul are working as a team. My body responds to the directives of my soul. This feeling is expressed by the last two verses of this psalm: *"Kol haneshamah tehallel Kah, Hallelukah; Kol haneshamah tehallel Kah, Hallelukah* — My entire soul praises God..."* My whole soul — my whole being — is flowing with song. I am one with the world.

The Radak comments on this verse:

> The soul contemplates the deeds of the Almighty, with the wisdom of the soul in accordance with its strength. While the soul is encompassed within the body, the body and the soul praise God.

Ibn Ezra quotes Rabbi Shlomo HaSephardi who explains the word *"kol"* (whole, entire), as follows: "This is a hint to the higher *neshamah*, the root of which is in the Heavens."

Rabbi Moshe Chaim Luzatto[33] explains that there are three parts of the soul in this world and two parts of the soul in the higher world. The three parts of the soul in this world correspond to three parts of the human psyche as follows:

> *Nefesh* — actions, deeds;
> *Ruach* — speech;
> *Neshamah* — thoughts.

The thoughts of an individual which emanate from the *neshamah* are translated into speech and action.

The three parts of the soul in this world have root sources in the higher worlds, namely:

> *Chayah* — life force or living essence; the experience of being within the realm of the Divine;[34]
> *Yechidah* — unique essence; the connection of my free will with the Almighty's Free Will.[35]

When the parts of my soul in this world are in harmony with their sources in the higher worlds, then I feel energized and connected. This wonderful feeling is the achievement of inner peace, however fleeting. The Hebrew word for peace, "*shalom*," comes from the Hebrew root *shalem* — which means "whole." This is the ultimate feeling I strive for. Don't we all? I'd like the feeling to occur more than once a year.

How can I achieve this "connected" feeling more often? By achieving a balance between body and soul. Just as I fuel and cater to the needs of my body, so too must I nourish my soul. I do this by plugging my three-part earthly soul into my two-part heavenly root soul, which in turn is connected to God. By "getting to know God" — by learning His will through the study of Torah, I can energize the root of my soul, which will in turn flow through a "trickle down" process into the three parts of my soul in this world.

How do I "get to know" how a contemporary author thinks? I read his works and thus gain an insight into his mind. I thereby feel as if I understand him. How do I get to know God? By reading His works — His Torah. In this way, I get to know how God expresses His will. My mind and soul can connect with my Source (God — the "Soul of souls"). With this realization ingrained in my psyche, I can carry this "energized" feeling with me wherever I go. It can happen more than once a year. It can happen every day.

When I am feeling positive about myself, I want my outer world to connect with my inner world. If I see a chair out of place at the dining room table, I'll put it back into place. I want the outer world to reflect my inner harmony.[36] I will be motivated to make my relationships and projects achieve a state of harmony with my inner sense of peace. In other words, when I am feeling good about myself I will give a lot of hugs. Inner peace, feeling *"shalem"* or "whole," is the key. Then *"kol haneshamah"* — my whole *neshamah*, in the lower and upper worlds — connect and fuse, and I can truly praise Hashem.

When the energy from the uppermost parts of my *neshamah* flows into the parts of the *neshamah* that are manifest within my body, there results a feeling of connectedness, of being "on." This itself is *"tehallel Kah"* — the greatest praise of Hashem — in that I am activating my full potential in my being an *eved Hashem*, a servant of God. As David HaMelech said: *"V'ani tefillah*[37] — I am a prayer,"* which means that my prayer to God is myself, my whole self, as I dedicate all of my God-given abilities in His service.

When I am in a positive mode I am in my most creative and productive state. I thus conclude the *Pesukei D'zimrah* with an inspiring awareness of the role of my *neshamah* in its service of God.

The Midrash tells us that the Almighty "looked into the Torah and created the World."[38] This means that God first established the eternal principles of truth, justice, and mercy, and then He embodied them in the Torah. Then He created the universe based on Torah principles, which makes the Torah the blueprint of Creation. Hashem used the spiritual forces that are found within the letters of the Hebrew alphabet contained in the Torah to create the different parts of the universe. If I want to connect my spiritual energy to Hashem, all I need to do is to put myself onto the same spiritual frequency which radiates from God. I can plug into God's spiritual frequency by following the Torah and by relating to Hashem through prayer. The evidence for this is that when I spend a few minutes learning Torah prior to davening, my prayer is much more meaningful and inspired.

With this psalm, the last psalm of David HaMelech's Book of Tehillim, we conclude *Pesukei D'Zimrah*. The name for God in this psalm is *"Kah"* — made up of the letter *yud* and the letter *hey*, which form the first half of God's ineffable Name — the tetragrammaton. The *yud* was used by Hashem to create the spiritual worlds, including *olam haba*. The *hey* was used by Hashem to create the physical worlds, including *olam hazeh*.

Hashem has implanted within me the mechanism with which He can relate to me, and I to Him. This medium is the *neshamah*, which has its source, the *"yud,"* in the spiritual world. By praising *"Kah"* I am able to connect with Hashem because I symbolize the *hey* of this world and I connect it with its source in the spiritual world. By praising Hashem I am injecting within my very being the highest form of self-awareness and self-validation.

The *hey* which was used to create me was culled from Yerushalayim — from the base of the *mizbeach* — the altar in the *Beis HaMikdash*. I was actually created from the material of *kedushah* — the holiness of the altar. It is on the altar that man offers a *korban* in order to came *karov* — close to his Creator. That is why the next part of the davening states:

בָּרוּךְ ה' מִצִּיּוֹן, שֹׁכֵן יְרוּשָׁלָיִם.

Bless Hashem out of Zion, Who dwells in Yerushalayim.

I can connect to my own Source in the higher world from my dwelling place in this world — the altar in Jerusalem, the point from which I was created. I can connect to my spiritual source by offering myself — my *tefillah* is myself — to my Source, Hashem.

ברוך ה׳ לעולם
Personal Redemption

In contrast to the wondrous feeling of the awareness of being "alive" and energized, I can feel, at times, overwhelmed, alienated, and alone against the world. The problems of daily living — of raising a family, making a living, and striving to find meaning in my life — can get me down. I can feel like I am in personal exile: exile from myself.

These next four verses from Psalms, according to Etz Yosef, refer to the overwhelming of the Jewish nation in their four exiles throughout history. The words follow the chronological history of the Jewish people, as follows:

1. *Elokei Yisrael* — God of Israel.

The Babylonian exile after the destruction of the First Temple caused us to cry in despair, as we describe in the psalm[39] which we say before *Birkas HaMazon* on a weekday: "There we sat and also wept when we remembered Zion...How can we sing the song of Hashem upon the alien's soil?"

And out of our despair, just as Hashem promised, He redeemed us from this first exile seventy years after the *churban*. And so we say *"Baruch Hashem Elokei Yisrael* — Blessed is Hashem, the God of Israel," since it is as a result of redemption from the degradation of Babylonian exile that the nations of the world witnessed the power of *Elokim* — the God of Israel — in guiding history and redeeming His people.

Not only is this true on a national level, it also speaks to me on a personal level. Even if I am in personal exile, brought about by my own mistakes, God promises to redeem me. If God redeemed my people notwithstanding the fact that their actions resulted in the destruction of the *Beis HaMikdash*, then certainly He can redeem me.

2. The national exile, namely the Persian exile, is referred to, as follows:

Oseh nifla'os levado — Who alone does wonders.

The wondrous act that God performed for us during this second exile was to allow Queen Esther to be held against her will in the palace of Achashverosh and still effect the redemption through her. The apparent tragedy of our Jewish queen imprisoned in the king's palace itself became the source for the redemption, as Esther's son Darius HaAcharon (Darius II) ordered that the Jews could resume building the Second Temple.[40] Only God, Alone, could have brought about such a miracle. It was clearly a moment of *"v'nahafoch hu"* — turnabout — bringing wondrous redemption from the midst of exile. As Shimshon said,[41] *"Me'az yavo masok* — out of the strong came forth sweetness."

3. The Redemption from the Greek exile under the Hellenists is alluded to with the words:

U'varuch Shem K'vodo l'olam — Blessed is His Glorious Name, forever.

The Greeks wanted the Jews to admit that by virtue of the overpowering dominant culture of Greece, the Jews no longer were able to claim "a portion in the God of Israel." It appeared that the darkness of Hellenism would mark the end of Judaism — but the light of redemption glowed from the Chanukah menorah as the Maccabees rededicated the Temple and reclaimed our inheritance as God's people. As such, we were still able to proclaim: "Blessed is His Glorious Name forever." Even when things seem darkest, if we trust in Hashem the light of Torah can redeem us.

4. The fourth and final future redemption is alluded to with the words:

> V'yimalei k'vodo es kol ha'aretz, Amen v'Amen — And may the earth be filled with His glory, Amen and Amen.

God's presence will be acknowledged by the entire world at the "end of days." Thus we say one Amen for the final redemption and the second Amen for the revival of the dead, which will occur at the end of the reign of the Mashiach.

Not only are the Jewish people worthy of redemption, but I too am worthy in God's eyes to be redeemed. If I want to activate even more of God's redemption, then I can seek out and make my unique contribution to the process of redemption by becoming more actively involved in Jewish observance and commitment. If I activate the relationship with God then it is more likely that He will provide me with the resources to enable me to make that contribution.

Can I actually make a significant contribution to the Jewish people and to the world? Isn't this egotistical thinking? Let me explain why I believe it is not. One Friday afternoon in November 1996, I visited my local barber shop, Lucas' Hair Salon in Bayswater, near my synagogue, which was one half mile from Kensington Palace. When I entered the shop I saw a lady who looked very much like Princess Diana. I turned to the man next to me and whispered: Is that the princess? He said he didn't know. (He turned out to be her security guard.) I saw a young girl run up to her and ask to take a photograph with her, which she declined. Then I knew it was her. Here was my big chance.

I said, "Princess, I am the rabbi of the local synagogue..."

The princess cut me off in mid sentence, "It appears that even rabbis can take off half an hour for a haircut."

I rose to the occasion. "It appears that even a princess can take off half an hour for a haircut!"

Eight months previously, I had written to the princess, inviting her to attend our synagogue's concert. I reminded her of this: "I invited the princess (I spoke in the third person out of respect for royalty) to my synagogue's Cantorial Concert for this coming Saturday night, but the princess was not able to join us."

"Thank you for inviting me," she said.

I said, "In Hebrew we say *chazak v'ematz* — Be strong and of good courage. I wish the princess well."

Just then I noticed a young teenager in the barber's chair next to the princess having mousse put in his hair. Only his hairdresser knows for sure that fourteen-year-old Prince William, the future king of England, puts mousse in his hair.

That night I came home after shul and told the story to my wife and children. "Can you believe it?" I said. "I sat in the very same chair as the future king of England. And guess what?" I said to my awe-inspired kids, "I'm also a king! It says in the Talmud: '*Yisrael b'nei melachim heim* — Israel are the sons of kings.' "[42]

We, the Jewish people, are sons and daughters of royalty. Avraham and Sarah, Moshe, David HaMelech...were all royalty. The essence of a king is that he provides for his subjects. Hashem is the King of kings, because He is the Ultimate Provider — of life itself. When I give charity or act with *chesed*, then I am acting Godlike — I am emulating God as a King. In this way, I can make my contribution to my spouse, my family, friends, and community. I can make a royal contribution to the world. It is not too idealistic. It is my obligation and my destiny to rise to the occasion and to live up to my royal status as a descendant of royal ancestors.

ויברך דויד
Self-Awareness

Just as God is singular, unique, and alone runs the world, I realize that I too am unique and alone as I journey through the adventures of life. With this realization in mind, now I am ready to really connect. I have now built, through the Songs of Praise, an acute sense of self-awareness. I realize that I am unique in God's eyes, just as Israel is unique as God's nation. From my newfound vantage point — a realization that I am a unique personality and a member of a unique people — I can truly extend my hand to the One Power and Ruler who can help me and guide me. I have put myself onto God's spiritual frequency — now I can really turn on the music.

וְהָעֹשֶׁר וְהַכָּבוֹד מִלְּפָנֶיךָ, וְאַתָּה מוֹשֵׁל בַּכֹּל, וּבְיָדְךָ כֹּחַ וּגְבוּרָה, וּבְיָדְךָ לְגַדֵּל וּלְחַזֵּק לַכֹּל.

Wealth and honor come from You and You rule everything — in Your hand is power and strength, and it is in Your hand to make anyone great or strong.

This is not a request or petition for strength. Rather, this is the ultimate praise of God. You strengthen and sustain everything, including me. I can actually "feel" the flow of Divine energy and life force flowing from God into my being in the midst of this realization. I am not merely saying words, I am feeling a closeness to the Source of my *neshamah*. My soul is warmed. My inner being feels an embrace from my Creator. My *neshamah* was created *b'tzelem Elokim* — in the image of God. When I daven these words, I try to focus on the most Godly or "God-like" part of my personality. I then allow that *nekudah hapenimis* (central core) of my being to receive life-affirming energy from Hashem — the "Soul of souls." I allow that feeling to spread throughout my being. When I recognize that I am a *kli* (vessel) to receive from Hashem, then my "self" becomes activated — truly "alive" — since I have been energized by the Source of life itself.

How can God give strength to everyone and everything simultaneously? The Iyun Tefillah puts the question beautifully by quoting a midrash[43] which states:

"*La'asos kir'tzon ish va'ish* — to do the will of every man." And yet how can this be? If two people seek to marry the same woman, can she possibly marry them both? If two ships set sail, and one pleads for a southerly wind while the other petitions for a northerly wind, can one wind guide them both? And if two men come before You, God — a Jew and his enemy — can You possibly satisfy the will of both? Is it not that one must be uplifted and the other despised? Who can satisfy the needs of *"kol ish va'ish"*? Only the Holy One, Blessed be He.

My task is not to understand the way God conducts the affairs of the world. Moshe asked God, "Show me your ways."[44] The Talmud[45] explains that Moshe was asking the ultimate question of philosophy: "Why does the good man suffer and the evil man prosper?" That question has crossed my mind on more than one occasion. I guess I am in good company if Moshe asked it 3300 years before me. Moshe was asking: "How do You, God, conduct the affairs of the world?" God answered: "No human can see my Face and live," which means that no man can understand Divine Providence. It is beyond human comprehension. If God wanted us to have this knowledge He would have granted it. Since He didn't, this is clearly one of the tests of faith that man has to endure in order to fulfill his destiny and purpose.

At the end of the *Amidah*, I sometimes beseech God and ask Him how I can grow as an *eved Hashem* from the particular ordeal I am going through. What Torah value or ideal can I better develop in my life or express as a result of or in response to my particular crisis? If I listen deeply to the music emanating from the depths of my inner being as I cleave to Hashem for guidance, I can sometimes intuit or hear myself answer my own question. Even though things aren't working out the way I had hoped or planned, Hashem is guiding me and asking me to confront a particular issue. He expects and urges me to deal with the issue and to grow from the experience. Here is where faith comes in. If things don't go my way, it is for a reason. It often turns out that I am glad my initial request wasn't granted. I work on my faith during davening by actively striving to trust that even though God didn't give me what I wanted, He did give me what I needed.

ויושע ה' ביום ההוא
Jewish Unity

וַיּוֹשַׁע ה' בַּיּוֹם הַהוּא אֶת יִשְׂרָאֵל מִיַּד מִצְרָיִם, וַיַּרְא יִשְׂרָאֵל אֶת מִצְרַיִם מֵת עַל שְׂפַת הַיָּם. וַיַּרְא יִשְׂרָאֵל אֶת הַיָּד הַגְּדֹלָה אֲשֶׁר עָשָׂה ה' בְּמִצְרַיִם, וַיִּירְאוּ הָעָם אֶת ה', וַיַּאֲמִינוּ בַּה' וּבְמֹשֶׁה עַבְדּוֹ.

And on that day, God delivered Yisrael from the hand of Mitzrayim, and Yisrael saw the Mitzrim dead on the seashore. And Yisrael saw the great hand which God wielded against Mitzrayim, and the nation feared God and believed in God and that Moshe was His servant.

The commentary *Bechor Shor* notes that in three places in this paragraph the Jewish people are described as "Yisrael." Once they saw that their oppressors had been killed, they experienced a metamorphosis from being the tribes or individuals of Yisrael into *"ha'am"* — the nation.

There are times in my spiritual "biorythm" that I feel alienated, isolated, and alone in the world. I get this feeling when I come into a gathering where I don't know anyone. It feels like its "me" and "them."

I become uneasily aware of my own precarious individuality. I feel self-conscious and vulnerable. It is sometimes equally felt when visiting a synagogue that I am not familiar with. The surroundings and people seem to blend into a unit into which I do not fit. However, if someone in the gathering or synagogue welcomes me, or begins chatting with me, or hands me a siddur, I feel my self-awareness merge with that person and perhaps even with the wider group. I feel drawn into the inner circle of the "community." I have changed from an individual "Israelite" into a member of the "nation."

The Jewish nation is unique in feeling a sense of kinship and camaraderie with a *"lansman"* — the Yiddish term for "fellow Jew." Have you ever been on holiday and met another Jew from a different country? Haven't you felt a sense of connection or security that you didn't feel before? It feels as if you've met a long-lost cousin — only you've never met him or her before.

The Jewish sense of "nationhood" is unique. How many of us demonstrated in the 60s and 70s for Soviet Jewry? Had I ever met Soviet Jews? No. But they were our brothers, and so we rallied and demonstrated. Have I ever met the Jews of Syria who were recently allowed to emigrate? No, but I give money for their absorption into Israel. Have I met the daughter of the chasid from Meah Shearim who collects money in my morning minyan for his daughter's wedding? No, but I give money to him, and I feel like I am participating in their *simchah*. I even say Mazel Tov. Imagine...I can figuratively dance at a Jerusalem wedding by contributing to this mitzvah of *hachnasas kallah* — assisting a bride. Do I personally know the Israeli soldiers killed by the suicide bomb in Netanya, or the elderly Jews murdered by a terror-ist attack in Istanbul, or the Jews murdered by a terrorist bomb in Buenos Aires? No, but I do feel their pain. I feel I have lost a family member. I am even moved to tears. I make private resolutions. I am going to do something more about my heritage. Their deaths move me to a greater sense of closeness to my people.

There is a story told of a rabbi who called upon a rich member of his community to solicit funds to buy coal for a poor widow to heat her home during the winter. The rabbi did not make the request for the donation until he left the rich man's home and stood outside saying goodbye in the freezing cold. Halachah requires a host to escort his guest at least six feet outside the door, to give the guest a sense of se-curity that the host truly enjoyed his company and is sorry to see him leave. The rich man did so without his coat, think-ing he would only be outside for a few seconds. The rabbi continued small talk with the rich man shivering outside. Then the rabbi asked for the donation. "Why didn't you ask me while we were inside?" asked the rich man. "I wanted you to feel what it meant to be cold, before you responded to my request," said the rabbi. The host identified with the widow's predicament, because he felt what she did. He then donated money to buy coal for all the poor people of the town.

This is called Jewish unity. Unity is not merely a theo-retical concept — it is a real and practical one. Jewish em-pathy drives a person to identify with the feelings of another. Jewish empathy is beyond sympathy. It is a willingness to act — to do a deed, a mitzvah — to connect oneself with one's fellow. The word "mitzvah" comes from the word "*tzeves*," which means "group" or "connection." When I perform a mitzvah I "connect" with God.

There are two tablets which make up the Ten Commandments. The first five deal with man's relationship with God (I am the Lord, Have no other gods...) and the next five deal with man's relationship with his fellowman (do not kill, commit adultery, steal, bear false witness, covet). I am looking for inner balance in my life — so I try to incorporate both sides of the tablets into my psyche. When I do a social mitzvah because God has commanded me to, then I synthesize and fuse both sides of the Ten Commandments in my soul — and feel a sense of inner *shleimus*.

Moshe grew up as an Egyptian prince in the house of Pharaoh. But he learned his spiritual heritage from his mother, Yocheved, who nursed and taught him. So we are not surprised to learn: "When Moshe grew up he went out among his brothers and saw their burdens."[46] Rashi teaches us that "Moshe grew up" refers to his physical maturity, and "he went out among his brothers" refers to his spiritual maturity.

To identify with the pain of others is to see beyond oneself — and to achieve a sense of connectedness to and love for one's neighbor. Moshe did more. He acted upon his feelings and he came to the aid of a Hebrew slave who was being beaten by an Egyptian taskmaster. He translated his sympathy into "identity." This is Jewish empathy: doing something about your feelings of compassion, by identifying yourself with your fellow to such an extent that you are "one" with him and you can't help but connect yourself to him.

I performed many weddings at the New West End Synagogue in London. I often shared the following story with my brides and grooms as they stood under the *chuppah*: The righteous man of Jerusalem, Rabbi Aryeh Levin, once accompanied his elderly wife to the doctor. When Rebbetzin Levin was called in to be examined, Rabbi Levin followed her into the consultation room.

"Rabbi," said the doctor, "your wife has been my patient for many years. You need not accompany her into the examination room."

"Doctor," said Rabbi Levin, "you don't understand. My wife's foot hurts us..."[47] Rabbi Levin so identified with his wife that he felt her joys and her pains. To become one emotionally integrated unit is the goal of marriage. So, too, albeit on a less intense level, must it be with our fellowmen, neighbors, and friends. I must begin to feel my neighbor's pain. Then I can begin the process of contributing to Jewish unity.

In January 1997, I attended a wedding in Gateshead, the famous Orthodox community in the north of England centered around the world famous Gateshead Yeshivah. I stayed at the home of Rabbi and Rebbetzin Yaakov Sipper, who coordinate the "*gemach*" or "*gemilus chesed*" (charity) funds for the community. If someone needs to borrow a folding bed, they go to a certain address. There are lending funds for baby car seats, cutlery, and cribs. You name it — they lend it. These types of lending facilities exist in almost every Orthodox community in Jerusalem and in many orthodox communities around the world. Such is the willingness of Jews to connect with others and to form a tangible and real community of unity.

The precedent for Jewish unity occurred when we left Mitzrayim and were forged into an eternal nation when we received the Torah on Har Sinai, as the Torah states: "And Israel encamped opposite the mountain."[48]

Rashi comments: *"K'ish echad b'lev echad* — as one man with one heart." The *Zohar* tells us that the Jewish people are really one *neshamah* — a collective soul.[49] According to the Maharal of Prague,[50] the Jewish nation gain a sense of *achdus* from the Unity of the Almighty. We feel close to and united with our fellow Jews because we are ambassadors of Hashem — Who is "One" and the "Unity" of the Universe. As the Talmud tells us:

> God said to Israel: "You made me a unique Entity in the world by saying, 'Hear O Israel, the Lord our God, the Lord is One,' and I will make you a unique entity in the world by saying, 'Who is like your nation Israel, one nation on earth."[51]

When we come together to pray in a minyan the Talmud tells us that the *Shechinah* comes to shul first and awaits the arrival of the minyan.[52] In a minyan our prayers are more easily answered, as God examines the good deeds of the entire group rather than paying microscopic attention to the deeds of each individual. Personal *kavanah* is better in a minyan. There is something special in knowing that my neighbor also needs Divine assistance. It reaffirms my sense of not being alone in the world. I feel a special strength that "we're in this together."

As we all stand silently together saying the private *Amidah*, there is a mysterious music in the silence of our individual prayers harmonizing as they travel from our hearts to God. The music comes from the fact that we represent the *"Am"* — the House of Israel. Whenever I feel like not getting up for morning minyan, I think of the symphony I might be missing. And to think I could be one of the musicians. In fact, if I don't get up for minyan the symphony literally won't sound the same. My presence or absence does make a difference.

אז ישיר משה
The Doing Makes You Ready

I hate having to make decisions, don't you? I am often faced with a choice whether to go back to an old project, job, or idea or to go forward into a new venture. If I go back, I know it will be hard going because I've "been there," but at least it has been "tried and true" — a known commodity. This is what is going through my mind: "I know what I have to face; maybe I should return and persevere? Or maybe I should go forward and try a new option. How do I know if I am doing the right thing?"

I may have no experience in the proposed new area of endeavor, but it does sound like an exciting opportunity. But what if I fail? Am I ready for it? Maybe my father's motto would apply: "the doing makes you ready." Only by "jumping in" and rolling up my sleeves will I become ready — by "making myself succeed."

This dilemma, which can apply to a myriad of life's challenges and decisions, is not new. The model originates with the Jewish people on the seventh day following the Exodus from Mitzrayim, as the Torah states:

> Mitzrayim pursued them and overtook them encamped by the sea — all the horses and chariots of Pharaoh, and his horsemen and army, by Pi-Hachiros before Ba'al Tzefon. Pharaoh approached; the children of Yisrael raised their eyes and behold, Mitzrayim was coming after them, and

Yisrael cried out to Hashem. They said to Moshe: "Were there no graves in Mitzrayim that you took us to die in the wilderness? What is this that you have done to take us out of Mitzrayim?"[53]

The Torah records the Israelites' reaction to this crisis:

Is not this the word that we did tell you already in Mitzrayim, saying: Let us alone, we would sooner serve the Mitzrim, for it is better for us to serve the Mitzrim than to die in the wilderness.[54]

When faced with the turbulent sea looming ahead, I, like the Israelites, might be inclined "to go back to Egypt" even if it means enslavement to "old masters." The root word of "Mitzrayim" is "*meitzar yom*" — which means "narrow straits." Egypt, as well as other old "taskmasters" or ideas, can put me in the mode of "narrow straits." The "sea" in spiritual terms means a place without apparent direction — formless and overwhelming. I sometimes have to decide whether to go back to old patterns — or whether I should go forward into exciting but uncharted waters.

For example, should I take that bold step by starting to keep Shabbos or telling my associate that I have decided to keep kosher outside my home as well? I could ask him to join me for our business lunch at a kosher restaurant. Should I open up my heart to my spouse and share my deepest secrets and aspirations? The way forward seems like I may be getting in "over my head." I may not be in control of the outcome, I may fail, I may be risking a lot. How do I decide whether to go forward or to "play it safe"?

Have you ever seen someone climb onto the swimming

pool's three-meter diving board for the first time and stand tentatively at the edge of the board with hands above head deciding whether or not to dive in? I've often wondered what the catalyst is, what is the "decisive" thought which immediately precedes someone's decision to leave the security of the board and to "dive" into something he or she has never done before.

I asked this question of my Rebbe when I was in the midst of my decision to leave my law practice and to go study for *semichah* in Yerushalayim. He answered by quoting the words of *Yedid Nefesh*, which we sing on *erev Shabbos* and at *shalosh seudos*: "*Nafshi cholas ahavasecha* — My soul yearns for your love."

I came to a point where my soul, my very being, craved growth, advancement, and development. I said to myself: "I cannot develop my character or personality if I stand still. I will risk the surety of dry land for the *simchah* that personality growth brings." And so, our diver on the three-meter board jumps into the water. And I moved to Yerushalayim.

ישתבח
Inspired Davening

This *berachah* of *Yishtabach* concludes the *Pesukei D'Zimrah* — the Songs of Praise. Before I petition Hashem for my needs in the *Shemoneh Esrei*, it is fitting for me to praise and acknowledge the greatness and power of the One who can grant me my requests. Thus, this *berachah* contains fifteen *shevachos* — praises of God:

1. *Shir* — song
2. *u'Shvachah* — and praise

3. *Hallel* — glorification

4. *v'Zimrah* — and hymns

5. *Oz* — strength

6. *u'Memshalah* — and dominion

7. *Netzach* — victory

8. *Gedulah* — greatness

9. *u'Gevurah* — and grandeur

10. *Tehillah* — praise

11. *v'Siferes* — and glory

12. *Kedushah* — holiness

13. *u'Malchus* — and sovereignty

14. *Berachos* — blessings

15. *v'Hodaos* — and thanksgiving

According to Avudraham, these fifteen forms of praise of Hashem correspond to the fifteen steps leading into the *Beis Hamikdash,* upon which the Levites stood and sang during the Temple service. These fifteen steps also correspond to the fifteen *"Shir Hama'alos"* (Songs of Ascent) written by David HaMelech,[55] which in turn correspond to the fifteen steps or stages that we go through in the Seder contained in the Haggadah of Pesach. Fifteen steps of praise which elevate us — and bring us to true, inner freedom.

The fifteen steps of the Temple, the fifteen Songs of Ascent, the fifteen praises of *Yishtabach,* and the fifteen stages of the Seder, have one common denominator — song. The first praise of *Yishtabach* is *"Shir"* — song. We begin to elevate ourselves through the song of the Levi'im as we enter the Temple to the melodies of inspiration. David HaMelech's fifteen songs are the link between the slavery of Egypt and the redemption at the Red Sea. If there is a song emanating from my *neshamah*, I can feel a sense of drive and motivation. I can only serve Hashem with enthusiasm if my psyche is in a state of song — expressing my inner appreciation for God's gift of life.

This is why my synagogue's daily morning minyan takes fifty minutes instead of the more standard twenty-eight minutes. We take the words of the *shacharis* service as a challenge. We see in the words an opportunity to joyously connect with God.

The words "*Yismichu hashamayim*" (Rejoice O' heavens), "*Hoshia es amecha*" (Redeem Your people), "*Malchuscha*" (Your kingdom [is everlasting]), "*L'El Baruch*" (to the Source, God), "*Emes v'Yatsiv*" (Truth and Strength), "*Tzur Yisrael*" (the Rock of Israel), are all sung joyously and passionately in our morning minyan. The voices of our minyan members blending in harmony serve to unite us, elevate us, and implant *shleimus* in our hearts, as we thank God for the opportunity of a new day of adventure in His service.

Only after experiencing the redeeming quality of singing the morning service have I come to understand the words of the end of *Yishtabach*, namely, "*Habocher b'shirei zimrah* — God, Who chooses songs of praise." We certainly become more uplifted in His service if we inspire ourselves to appreciate the gift of witnessing a new dawn. How can I but say the words "*Yismichu hashamayim* — Rejoice O' heavens"; I must sing them with a *nigun*, a melody. Let my heart feel what my mouth is saying. It is a great kindness on the part of Hashem that He "chooses" Songs of Praise for me to use. He allows, urges, and challenges me to rise to the challenge of achieving my potential in this forthcoming day by serving Him from a perspective of *shirei zimrah*. Since God is "with me" in my difficulties — as it states, *"Imo Anochi b'tzarah,"* "I am with him in his pain"[53] — then He is surely "with me" in my joy as I rejoice in Him.

On an ultimate level God is *"Ga'oh Ga'ah —* Exalted beyond all exaltations." Since He is the *"Ein Sof,"* the "Infinite Being," nothing that finite man can say can come anywhere near to adequately praising God, or cause Him to be happier with one prayer than with another. On this level of my relating to God, all praise is gross in its falseness, since God is beyond description or praise. My *shacharis* prayers sung with the greatest intensity are simply inadequate to praise the Creator of the Universe.

On a different level, however, there is room for me to feel that God derives more "pleasure" from a joyous *shacharis* than from a mumbled one. On the level that God allows me to interact with Him, where He opens Himself or reveals Himself to me, then in that sense I can make an offering which is a *"re'ach nichoach —* a sweet smelling offering" to God. In the ultimate scheme of things my actions and prayers can have no effect on God, per se. In this second, relationship aspect, however, where God opens Himself up to me in the sense that He has hopes and plans for me — then my actions and prayers can and do make an "impression" on Him. If I intensify myself in His service, surely He is more "moved" than if I serve Him with less feeling. My goal in prayer should be to reach a level which is described in the song *"Lecha Dodi"* that we sing Friday night, namely: *"Yasis alayich Elokaich, kimsos chassan al kallah —* Your God will rejoice over you, like a groom rejoicing over his bride."

If your morning minyan seems to be sending its prayers heavenward by "fax," a twenty-eight minute, supersonic "Concorde" minyan, it is time to introduce an earlier start to the minyan and a happier, melodic davening. The minyan should decide on *nigunim* they like and introduce a few into the davening. Imagine the feeling of leaving for work in the morning with a melody playing in your mind. Whenever you face a trying moment you will be able to hear that *nigun* playing as background music and can perhaps approach the problem from the perspective of that *shacharis* melody.

I can thus conclude *Yishtabach* with a truly meaningful expression of the words *"Baruch Chei Ha'olamim* — Blessed is the Life Force of the Universe." When I say these words after a few songs of praise, I can actually feel the life force come alive within me. When I say God is blessed, I am surely not adding anything to God. He certainly does not need my blessing, since He is already perfect. When I say God is the *"Chei Ha'olamim,"* I am saying that He is the Source — the Generator of my life energy. According to Nefesh Hachaim,[54] Hashem "receives" my blessing, thereby allowing me a moment of connection or *deveikus* with Him.

Now, I am ready to approach the central part of the davening, the *shacharis* itself. The *Chatzi Kaddish* signals the end of this section of the morning service.

NOTES

1. Tehillim 104:24.
2. Lawrence Keleman, *Permission to Believe* (Southfield, Michigan: Targum Press, 1990), 48–50.
3. 5:1.

4. Bereishis 2:5.

5. Rabbeinu Bachya ibn Paquda, *Chovos HaLevavos, Sha'ar Avodas HaElokim*, Introduction, ch. 3; *Sha'ar Cheshbon HaNefesh*, 3:16.

6. Rabbi Dr. Dovid Gottlieb, Ohr Somayach, Jerusalem.

7. Rabbi Eliyahu Dessler, *Michtav MiEliyahu*, vol. 1, p. 155.

8. Rabbi Samson Raphael Hirsch, *The Pentateuch — Translation and Commentary* (Gateshead: Judaica Press, Ltd., 1982), 27:22.

9. Bereishis 32:5.

10. Ibid. 29:11.

11. Shmuel II 24.

12. My *teshuvah* is valid even if I am never tested with this transgression. If I am tested and succeed, this achieves *teshuvah gemurah*. We should not look to be tested, however, in order to achieve *teshuvah gemurah*. Hashem will send tests that He deems appropriate. See Rabbi Dr. Dovid Gottlieb's *The Informed Soul* (New York: Mesorah Publications, Ltd., 1990), pp. 179–195.

13. Bereishis 42:21.

14. Ibid. 44:16.

15. Ibid. 37:26–27.

16. Gottlieb, *The Informed Soul*, p. 185. Even if the test failed, there is still a process of spiritual growth created in those aspects of the process from which the individual did learn and grow.

17. *Hashem Melech* (Tehillim 10:16), *Hashem Malach* (Ibid. 93:1), *Hashem Yimloch* (Shemos 15:18).

18. Joseph B. Soloveitchik, *The Lonely Man of Faith* (New York: Doubleday, 1965), 37–42, 79.

19. "*Taryag*" is a mnemonic, the numerical value of which is 613.

20. *Berachos* 4b.

21. Ibid.

22. *Michtav MiEliyahu, Kuntrus HaBechirah*, vol. 1, p. 117.

23. Rabbi Chaim of Volozhin, *Nefesh HaChaim, sha'ar alef*, ch. 12.

24. "Who Will Be the Zaidys of Our Children," song by the Megama Duo.

25. *Eitz Yosef.*

26. Soloveitchik, *The Lonely Man of Faith*, p. 41.

27. *Michtav MiEliyahu*, vol. 4, pp. 98–102.

28. Rabbi Moshe Chaim Luzatto, *Derech Hashem*, part 2, ch. 3.

29. Tehillim 55:23.

30. Shemos 20:18.

31. *Shabbos* 133b.

32. Mishlei 14:28.

33. *Derech Hashem*, part 1, ch. 2.

34. Aryeh Kaplan, *Inner Space* (Jerusalem: Moznaim Publishing Corporation, 1991), 19.

35. Ibid., 20.

36. *Michtav MiEliyahu*, vol. 1, *Diglei Midbar, Yesh Seder Leshem Seder*, p. 92.

37. Tehillim 109:4.

38. *Bereishis Rabbah* 1:1.

39. Tehillim 137.

40. Rashi, *B'Shnas Shtaim L'Darvyavesh*, *Megillah* 15a, comments that Darius II, son of Queen Esther and Achashveirosh, allowed the Jews to resume construction of the Second Temple after it had been halted for eighteen years by the Shomronim (Samaritans), work which had been started during the reign of Cyrus.

41. Shoftim 14:14.

42. *Shabbos* 67b.

43. *Megillas Rabbah*, Megillas Esther 1:8.

44. Shemos 33:13.

45. *Berachos* 7a.

46. Shemos 2:11.

47. Simcha Raz, *A Tzaddik in Our Time — the Life of Rabbi Aryeh Levin* (Jerusalem: Feldheim Publishers, 1989), 150.

48. Ibid. 19:2.

49. *Beis HaMedrash*, Aharon Yalink, ed. (Jerusalem, 1938), ch. 6, p. 84.

50. See his commentary *Gur Aryeh*, on the words *"Havah nis'chakmah lo"* ("Let us outsmart him") in Shemos 1:10.

51. *Chagigah* 3a.

52. *Berachos* 6a.

53. Shemos 14:9–11.

54. Ibid. 14:12.

55. Tehillim, chs. 120–134.

56. Ibid. 91:15.

57. *Sha'ar Beis*, ch. 4.

Chapter 3

SHEMA AND ITS BERACHOS

יוצר אור ובורא חשך
The Big Picture

I find it extremely difficult to "pray inspired" when things are not going well. I may have a sore throat, my kids might not be cooperating, and my work may simply not be progressing smoothly. So what do I have to be happy about or thankful for? My mother tells me, "Well, Yisroel, just chalk that one up to experience." "But Mom," I reply, "I've got enough chalk to last a lifetime." So how can I daven joyously when I'm drowning in a sea of chalk?

The first *berachah* we say after *Barechu* is *Yotzer ohr, u'Vorei choshech* — Hashem forms light and creates darkness. The Talmud[1] tells us that we are required to mention "daytime during the night and nighttime during the day." The *Yalkut Yeshayah* explains that it is necessary to mention that God is the source of both darkness and light to counter the philosophy of the Zoroastrians, who suggest that darkness or evil, and light or goodness, emanate from two separate sources, the Bad Source and the Good Source (or, in

Chinese philosophy, the yin and yang). This anti-monotheist ideology presupposes that there is a god of light, goodness, and truth and that there is an anti-god (God forbid) which is the source of darkness, evil, and falsehood.

When I begin the *shacharis* service with this blessing, I reaffirm my faith that Hashem is the Sole Source of good and evil, and that evil is merely placed in the world as an "angel" or servant of God to serve His overall plan. It is Hashem who establishes the parameters of the positive and negative forces in the world, the *yetzer tov* (positive inclination) and the *yetzer ra* (negative inclination). God uses the negative inclination to push me to use my positive inclination. Both inclinations are of necessity placed within me in order to allow me free will to choose the proper path to thus earn a reward. Hashem sees the Big Picture — and is *Oseh Shalom*, the One who makes peace or "wholeness" from what seem to be opposing forces. Hashem creates everything — *"u'Vorei es hakol."* In this *berachah* I demonstrate my trust in Hashem, that He causes the bad and good to come together for my ultimate good.

Let me share a simple example. My family used to live in the West End of London in the Bayswater area not far from Hyde Park. My girls attended Beis Yaakov and my boys attended Torah Temimah School, which are located in the Jewish area, a thirty-minute car ride, followed by a further thirty-minute school bus ride for the kids to get to their schools. I am sure you are familiar with the flurry of activity that is necessary to get kids out to school in the morning; a challenge at best, chaos usually.

My shul minyan started at 7:00 A.M. and concluded at 8.00 A.M. In order to get my kids to their respective buses so that they could arrive at school on time and I could make my first appointment, I had to leave home no later than 8:05. But kids are kids, and sometimes they are not ready to go — such that I would miss their buses and have to drive them to their respective schools, which would get them there late and make me miss my first appointment.

At first, I was frustrated at this situation and was unable to understand or appreciate God's *chesed* and love for me in adding ninety minutes to my morning journey and making us all late. But when I allowed myself a glimpse at the Big Picture and let go of my anger and frustration, I began to see the *chesed* of Hashem. One day, after driving my daughter to school late, I watched from the school gate as my eight-year-old daughter entered the school and took the hand of a four-year-old child who was also arriving late. I watched as my daughter bent down to the little girl, asked if she was all right, put an arm around her, and guided her into the school. This display of *chesed* on the part of my daughter touched me deeply. Had I caught the bus on time, my daughter would not have been given the opportunity of doing this *chesed*, and I would not have been privileged to witness it.

If only I could learn to be patient with Hashem and the events with which He presents me, I would be able to witness the Big Picture and see the love and *chesed* of Hashem on a regular basis. If I am patient and keep my eyes and soul open, then I will eventually see the "light" emerge from the midst of the apparent "darkness." Sometimes I cannot possibly see the kindness unless I am strong enough to first go through the challenge of the darkness. Nesivos Shalom explains that is why each Jewish day begins at sundown, as the

Torah states in Bereishis: "*Vayehi erev vayehi voker* — And it was evening and it was morning..." We must first work through the challenge of darkness and "evening" and only then arrive at clarity, light, and "morning."

Thus, Hashem is the Creator of *ohr* (light) and *choshech* (darkness). The difficulties and the kindnesses that Hashem presents us with come from the same source — God Himself. What appears to be evil is merely a hidden kindness. It is my job to "hang in there" and to weather the challenge of the superficial cover of darkness until the light appears. It is also God's challenge of my faith to see whether I can extract the good from the midst of the darkness.

The Iyun Tefillah quotes a midrash[2] on the verse in Bereishis: "And God saw all that He had created and, behold, it was very good."[3]

> Said Rav Huna: "And behold it was good" — this refers to the Attribute of Goodness; "And behold it was very good" — this refers to the Attribute of Trials and Suffering.
>
> Rav Zeirah said: "And behold it was good" — this refers to the Garden of Eden; "And behold it was very good" — this refers to Gehinom (the twelve-month process of soul purification following death).
>
> Said Rav Shmuel the son of Yitzchak: "And behold it was good" — this refers to the Angel of Life; "And behold it was very good" — this refers to the Angel of Death.

The Iyun Tefillah makes the meaning clear. He teaches that the word "good" is mentioned in connection with our ability to perceive God's Divine goodness directly. The phrase "very good" is mentioned in connection with our inability to see God's goodness directly; rather, our understanding that some things (i.e., suffering, death) contribute to the good indirectly, known as general Divine Providence. In this way we can appreciate that "everything is good," even those things which are not apparently good to the individual observer.

When a specific event or challenge is presented to me, I am usually too wrapped up in dealing with the issues at hand to appreciate why the challenge is occurring. I am unable to put the crisis into perspective. This important lesson, taught to us by the verse in Bereishis and referred to in *shacharis*, urges us to take one step back from the situation and put the event into context. If I would be able to "switch into" the Big Picture mode, in some fashion attempt to see the world from God's perspective, then I would have a broader lens with which to analyze the event and to begin to see what it is that God "wants from me" by presenting me with this particular challenge.

HaRav Elchanan Wasserman, *zt"l*, tells the following parable,[4] which he related in the last days of his life before he was murdered by the Nazis. A city resident, on his first trip to a farm, watched as a farmer walked through his ripening golden wheat fields and began to harvest the wheat. He took kernels of a stalk of wheat and placed the grains into newly ploughed soil. "How could you take such beautiful grain and bury it in the ground?" asked the visitor. "Just wait and see," said the farmer. In time the seeds grew into stalks of wheat and the visitor watched the wheat being harvested once again. This time the kernels were taken to the mill and the visitor watched as they were milled into flour. "How could you destroy those beautiful kernels?" demanded the city man. "Just wait and see," replied the farmer. The flour was mixed with water and the dough kneaded and placed into the oven. "How could you even contemplate burning such beautiful dough in the oven?" complained the city slicker. "Just wait and see," said the farmer. The dough baked into fine bread, and the farmer presented the city man with a steaming loaf of fresh bread. "You must have patience at each stage," said the farmer, "if you are unfamiliar with the production process."

When God presents me with a painful challenge, I am only looking through a symbolic keyhole into the room as I try to understand the reason for the challenge. God, however, sees the overall plan of the building and thus sees the Big Picture. I have to step out of my "keyhole" mode when I feel the kernels of my life being crushed in the mill of life experience. I must try to look beyond my egocentric world view since I am not familiar with the overall harvesting, planting, reaping, milling, kneading, and baking processes of my life. I can only comprehend one of these processes at a time. I must train myself to be patient and to heed the Farmer's message — "Just wait and see."

People often ask me, "Why doesn't God speak to us like He did to Avraham and Sarah? If only He could speak to me, I too would become religious." I answer with some trepidation: "He does speak to us today. Through the events that happen to us, God is guiding, directing, and encouraging us to grow. He has also given us a Torah to use as a guide and framework, to respond to the events which He presents to us. The Torah does not provide a directive for our required response to every situation in detail, but in the principles of the Torah we can find a general *mehalach* — pathway — which we can use to guide us to an appropriate response to God's challenges.

וּבְטוּבוֹ מְחַדֵּשׁ בְּכָל יוֹם תָּמִיד מַעֲשֵׂה בְרֵאשִׁית.

In His goodness He renews daily, perpetually, the work of Creation.

When I was a teenager, I asked my bar mitzvah teacher, Rabbi Daniel Mund of Montreal, simple quiz questions like: "What is the purpose of life? What am I doing here?" He wisely told me that I was asking for the "blueprint of creation," and only God could tell me the architectural plans He has in store for me. I would have to figure out my purpose in life, over time, on my own, my Rebbe advised.

When I left law school and began to work in a law firm in Toronto, I began to formulate an answer to the "purpose of life" question by virtue of my resolve to maintain consistency in my work, and to "keep going" despite the hurdles that were put in my way. The purpose of life, I figured then, was to "get up in the morning and to keep going" toward my goal of closeness to Hashem and fulfillment of my potential. The constancy, perseverance, and resilience necessary to keep plugging away at my job during the day and my studies at the yeshivah at night, gave me a sense of security, direction, and purpose.

The fact that I can observe consistency and constancy in nature gives me a sense of security as well. The fact that Hashem sustains nature consistently and constantly "speaks to me" and challenges me to "hang in there" and to keep going on an even keel. My father encourages me by comparing life to driving along the highway. If I maintain a firm but flexible grip on the steering wheel — remembering to access my personal abilities, talents, and resources — then I can withstand the potholes, bumps, and curves that I encounter on the highway of life. I just keep going over, through, and around the obstacles by drawing upon my personal strengths. The obstacle in my way may disorient my sense of direction, but I must try to maintain my focus and inner confidence that I have the innate abilities and personal resources to steer through this challenge.

I feel enveloped within a warm feeling of security when I say the words: *"HaMechadesh b'tuvo b'chol yom tamid maaseh bereishis* — Who renews daily, perpetually, the work of Creation."

Hashem is not only the *Borei* — Creator — but also the *Manhig* — the Sustainer and Director of the Universe. The Etz Yosef explains that is why we say in *Baruch She'amar,* *"Baruch Oseh Bereishis"* — Blessed is the One who creates the world anew, every day. The world is an ongoing state of creation, as Hashem recreates the world "ex nihilo" — out of nothing — every second. Hashem sustains and energizes every molecule of Creation every second.[5] If Hashem would stop "willing" anything or anyone in the world "to be" then it would "be" no longer.

When I contemplate the fact that Hashem has willed me to live this morning, by returning my *neshamah* to me, and by sustaining me in life, I gain a sense of personal self-confidence in the knowledge that Hashem has confidence in me, and that I have a continuing role to play in His world. If He has confidence in me shouldn't I have confidence in myself?

אֵל בָּרוּךְ גְּדוֹל דֵעָה הֵכִין וּפָעַל זָהֲרֵי חַמָּה.

The Blessed God, Who is great in knowledge,
prepared and worked on the rays of the sun.

When I was fifteen years old, Herzliah High School of
Montreal organized a study tour of Israel for our
ninth-grade class. We spent five months studying near Jerusalem, in Ramat Shapira in Moshav Beit Meir, overlooking
the Judean Hills. When I witnessed my first sunset over the
mountains, I was moved and inspired. The sometimes orange,
sometimes red sun seemed to beckon to me as it set quickly on
the Judean horizon. It was my first encounter with the awesome and transcendent power of the Creator. As I would
watch the majestic sun tucking smoothly behind the hills,
something awakened within my soul!

This first *berachah* before *Shema Yisrael* is called
Birchas Hayotzer — the Blessing of Creation. It praises God
as Creator of the spiritual system with its heavenly angels,[6]
namely those agents which God employs to conduct the
business of the universe, including the natural forces, the
planets, the galaxies, the sun, and the moon.

I have always wondered what the planetary system had
to do with me, in particular. How can I relate to a blessing
about the sun and moon? The commentator Rabbi Baruch
Halevi Epstein, in his book *Baruch She'amar*, explains that
just as the sun is necessary for physical life to exist on earth,
so is it necessary for my spiritual sustenance on earth as
well.

Let us contemplate the fact that even a slight change in
the distance between the sun and earth would result in life

not being sustainable on earth.[7] In reflecting on this fact, I have two possible options. I may feel that this phenomenon is a result of an accident or randomness. If so, I am forced into the position that this planet and I are here by virtue of a quirk of random statistical improbability, thereby rendering my presence in the universe accidental and ultimately purposeless. If the world is an accident of nature and was not put here by design, then everything within the world, including me, is here by accident and has no ultimate purpose. After all, how can I have any greater purpose than the universe itself, within which I find myself?[8] On the other hand, I may conclude that this wondrous phenomenon was designed by God with mankind in mind, including me. I marvel at how all of the cosmic, galactic, and planetary systems are structured perfectly in order to sustain life on this planet, including me. Thus, the sun and moon have everything to do with me.[9]

Ultimately, however, even if I don't want to believe that my existence is meaningless, even if I feel that I do have a purpose, this may emanate from a personal desire to feel meaningful, which would ultimately be self-serving and certainly unverifiable. The real reason I have meaning and purpose is because God has told me I have a purpose, which is "to serve Him and to follow His commandments."

Concerning the fourth day of Creation, the Torah states:

> And Elokim said: "Let there be luminaries in the skies of the Heavens to differentiate between the day and the night, and they will be as signs for the seasons, days, and years."[10]

Rashi comments as follows:

The sun was established by God to regulate the seasons and thus to establish the Festivals of Pesach in springtime, Shavuos in summertime, and Sukkos in the autumn. The moon was established by Hashem to regulate the months and thus the dates of the Festivals.

I can relate to God through responding to the changing seasons by going up to Jerusalem on the *Shalosh Regalim* (three Festivals — Pesach, Shavuos, Sukkos). I can relate to God by responding to the new moon after the *Beis Din* (Jewish Court sitting in Jerusalem) declares a new month. Thus, with the advent of each new month I have an opportunity to renew myself as I pursue my life's mission of coming closer to my Creator. This concept of responding to the changing seasons and months trains me to be an active participant in the unfolding of the world. Through these cosmic phenomena God is speaking to me, inviting me to witness the astronomical events of the world unfold around me, inviting me to respond and to interact with the world. I have an active role to play in the world by observing the *me'oros* (luminaries) and by initiating my personal response, as part of the Jewish people, by celebrating Rosh Chodesh and the Festivals.

Even on a daily basis the sun and moon "speak" to me. The sunrise tells me it is time to adventure and experience a new day. The *neitz*, or dawn elicits a halachic response — I daven *shacharis*.[11] The "*shekiah*," the setting sun, speaks to me and asks me to contemplate how I am doing in achieving my day's objectives. Despite the frantic pace of the day and all of my activities, I have an opportunity to pause and touch base with God and relate my accomplishments to Him. I respond to the setting of the sun by standing in *Amidah*[12] — to thank Hashem for allowing me to work for Him today. As God closes the curtain on the day, I hand back my day's accomplishments to my Creator, as a messenger reports to the one who sent him.[13]

The appearance of three stars invites me to daven *maariv* and to reflect on my overall behavior that day to see where I can make course adjustments and corrections.

Thus, the seasons, the new moon, and the daily rising and setting sun invite me to participate in the process of the world by keeping my finger on my own pulse and on the pulse of the Jewish people through my observance of the mitzvos. In contemplating the *me'oros* I gain a sense of belonging — that I belong in God's cosmos and that He wants me to respond to the luminaries' movements halachically, through prayer, and through the observance of Shabbos and the Festivals.

One *erev* Shabbos on my Herzliah High School trip in Israel, I also experienced a different type of spiritual moment. Our group attended Friday night services in Ramat Shapira's synagogue. There we were, thirty-seven fifteen year olds and a few *madrichim*, singing *"Lecha Dodi"* — the sixteenth-century Kabbalistic song that we sing to welcome the Shabbos Queen. For some reason, all of us were "into it" that night, and the sound that carried over the Judean Hills was moving and emotional. I was so moved by the power of the song that I stopped for a moment to listen to the arrival of Shabbos. As I sat silently at the back of the small shul I remember saying to myself: "Can this possibly be the music coming from forty voices? It can't be. It sounds like four hundred voices. Maybe the angels are singing with us?" And then, I remember the feeling and the precise moment which began to change my life, when I asked myself: "Could there be something to this Judaism stuff?" I rejoined the voices. Some time later, I answered my own question when I wrote my parents a letter saying that I decided that I did not want to drive on Shabbos anymore.

וְכֻלָּם מְקַבְּלִים עֲלֵיהֶם עֹל מַלְכוּת שָׁמַיִם זֶה מִזֶּה.

Then they all accept upon themselves the yoke of Heavenly sovereignty from one another.

Contrary to popular belief, Judaism is an upbeat, dynamic, and joyous way of life. If so, then what's all this about *"ol malchus Shamayim"* — the yoke of Heaven? This statement hardly fosters a feeling in me that my service of Hashem is "upbeat, dynamic, and joyous." Rather the "yoke" or burden of Heaven seems to perpetuate the old Sunday morning *cheder* stereotype of an overbearing, boring, and "downer" religion.

The answer lies not in the definition of "yoke" but in its purpose. A yoke is placed on an animal, i.e., an ox, not to burden it but to guide it and assist it in fulfilling its purpose — which is to plough the field. If the animal were not harnessed, it would be easily distracted and fail to fulfill its purpose — to serve man by ploughing the field.

Let us apply this analysis to ourselves. Many people feel that the purpose of life is to "enjoy life," to "eat, drink, and be merry for tomorrow we die."[14] As a result of this attitude I may secure for myself a measure of physical stimulation and sensual gratification, but after a few years of "joling" (in

South Africa), "cruising" (in North America), or "having a brilliant time" (in England), I stop and wonder what I have really accomplished or achieved in substantive terms. I can't build upon yesterday's physical experiences nor develop a philosophy of personal growth through living a life of immediate sensual gratification. For example, I can't enjoy yesterday's steak a second time. Once I've tasted it, it is gone. In addition, yesterday's steak will not add to the pleasure of today's steak — sensual pleasure is not cumulative. Spiritual experiences and personal character growth, however, can be built upon and developed so that I can achieve a greater sense of meaning and accomplishment.[15]

The 1960s was the generation of rebellion — campus sit-ins and "hippyism." The 1970s was the "me" generation — looking out for "number 1." The 1980s was the greed and junk bond generation. What about the 1990s and millenium? Now that we have experienced life in the "fast lane" and found ourselves still unfulfilled, I believe the millenium minded generation are seeking meaning in life and values. They are seeking direction, guidance, and spiritual fulfillment.

The "*ol malchus Shamayim,*" the yoke of Heaven, is the general philosophy of Judaism as a "way of life" — which guides and directs me, to allow me to achieve my goal and unique mission in life. I express this general "*ol*" of "serving Heaven" via the *ol Torah*, the yoke of Torah, and the *ol mitzvos*, the yoke of the commandments. These guidelines, which are subsumed under the general philosophy of the "yoke of Heaven," provide a framework within which I can strive toward the purpose of life, *kirvas Elokus* — coming close to God.

I express my striving to come close to God and His standards by working on my character and developing my personality. If I want to connect with God and elevate myself to His values, I will follow the *"ol"* — direction of Torah and mitzvos — and live within a purpose-built system that guides me toward fulfilling my destiny.

No matter how estranged a Jew has become from Judaism, he or she still feels a special connection to the Pesach Seder. The word *"seder"* means "order" — we follow the Haggadah which sets out a framework of fifteen steps to commemorate our Exodus from Egypt some 3300 years ago. There is a famous question asked about the Seder. Why should I celebrate the Jewish people's holiday of national freedom from Egypt with a "Seder" — a set order of service? Isn't this a paradox? Why not allow me to celebrate Jewish national liberation through a creative expression of personal freedom? Why can't I celebrate by dancing with an Israeli flag as I run around Hyde Park singing at the top of my lungs? Why isn't the joy over our national freedom allowed to be expressed in any way the spirit moves me?

The reason is that the Seder service provides me with guidelines within which I can follow in the footsteps of my ancestors; I can follow the Haggadah proudly, knowing that Jews all around the world are following the same service. I can, in this way, connect with the underlying unity of the Jewish people in my service of God. Freedom without direction leads to anarchy. True freedom is attained through a framework within which I can express my creative self and fulfill my destiny within a purposeful system.

בְּנַחַת רוּחַ...

With tranquility...

These two words express my deepest hope and aspiration. I would like to get sufficiently good at the "art of living" so that I can go through my day *"b'nachas ruach"* — in a state of "spiritual tranquility." When I was learning in Israel and walked to Ohr Somayach Yeshivah through Meah Shearim and Bucharim every morning, I experienced a sense of *"nachas ruach"* — serenity. Walking through the narrow, winding paths with the sounds of *cheder* children singing their morning prayers flowing over me, I experienced a sense of inner calm — inner peace.

How can I recreate this sense of inner tranquility as I journey through the hectic pace of "real" life. The answer, I believe, lies in the words which precede *"b'nachas ruach"* — which are *"l'hakdish l'Yotzram* — to sanctify their Creator."* If I walk through my "fast lane" life with an underlying confidence and trust that with every step and action I am serving and can serve my *"Yotzer,"* my Creator, then I can generate within my psyche an inner sense of peace, notwithstanding and despite the external challenges which attempt to upset my state of inner equilibrium. The secret is knowing that whatever God sends my way is out of His *chesed* and love for me. Through the events and challenges I experience along life's journey, God is guiding me and relating to me in order to teach me something.

Let's go back to my morning "shlepp" to catch my kids' school buses, for example.

I was so upset each time I would miss the kids' buses

that it would virtually ruin my morning. On one trip, after missing the bus yet again, my five-year-old son saw me trying to compose myself and said: "Daddy, I know why you're not upset — because now you can spend more time with us!" I froze in my tracks! He was right. I smiled, calmed down, and started "shmoozing" with the kids about school, friends, homework, and roadwork. And I actually enjoyed it. Thank God I missed the bus!

These days when I miss the bus, I say to myself: Okay, Hashem, I know I missed the bus for a reason — I have to learn something from my kids or about them. Invariably, one of my kids comes up with a comment or asks a question that "blows me away." Now I believe I understand the Talmudic statement of *"Kol d'ovid rachmana l'tav ovid"* — all that is done by Hashem is for the good.

I used to think that this was a mere rationalization. But, taking a fresh look at the famous Gemara about Rabbi Akiva,[16] we can see that it is not a rationalization but a positive reality. The Talmud relates that Rabbi Akiva was traveling with a donkey, a rooster, and a torch through the countryside, but was refused entry to a particular town to lodge for the night. He had to sleep on the outskirts of the town. A lion came and killed his donkey, a wolf came and killed his rooster, and the wind blew out his torch. Rabbi Akiva did not get angry with God; rather, he said, *"Kol d'ovid rachmana l'tav ovid"* — all that is done by Hashem is for the good. In the morning he learned that bandits had come to the town at night and killed the inhabitants.

It was a good thing he had not been admitted to the town. It was a blessing that his animals were killed, for had they made noise the bandits might have found him as well.

And it was a *berachah* that his torch was blown out so that Rabbi Akiva was not seen. It is not a rationalization to say that whatever happens is "for the best." It is a reality that it is *actually* better that it happened this way. It *had* to happen this way. It is up to me to do my best to make sure that I am well protected and that I act wisely in my affairs — but if the unexpected happens, it is my reaction which can lead me either to inner turmoil or to inner calm.

The events and challenges that I am presented with are up to God. My reaction to them and what I learn from these events are up to me. It is my job to extract the good from a particular event and to seek out that which God wants me to learn from a particular "crisis" or challenge.

כִּי הוּא לְבַדּוֹ פּוֹעֵל גְּבוּרוֹת...

For He alone effects mighty deeds...

There are eight phrases with which we praise God in this *berachah*:

1) *Po'el gevuros* — "effects mighty deeds." 2) *Oseh chadashos* — He "makes new things." Hashem effects mighty deeds in that He sustains every particle in the universe, because He created everything "*yesh mi'ayin* — something from nothing*" (creation ex nihilo). If Hashem would stop "thinking" about any aspect of the world for one second, a vacuum would be created in that thing because God's Life Force would no longer be sustaining it — it would thus disappear.[17]

I can now apply this concept to the manner in which God sustains me personally as part of the universe. If I concentrate on the intake of air as I breathe (my *neshimah*, breath), I can actually feel Hashem's hand sustaining me (my *neshamah*, soul) in life, and I realize that by virtue of my existence in the world I have intrinsic worth, since God bothers to "think" about me and sustain me in life. I must be important enough to God's plan to be sustained by Him. I am encouraged and strengthened by this knowledge and gain a sense of value knowing that I am in God's thoughts.

3) *Ba'al milchamos*, 4) *Zorea tzedakos* — Hashem is "Master of wars, Who sows kindnesses." Not only is God the Master of international history and wars among nations, He is also Master of my personal wars and challenges. When I am faced with difficulties and crises, the world appears to be standing in opposition to me. From the midst of my troubles, and precisely as a result of being tested, I try to weather the storm, and hopefully emerge with a sense of personal growth and character development. It is precisely because there are crises and problems in life that I am pushed to rise above myself.

Isn't it true that only when we are pushed to the seeming limits of our capabilities do we bring out the best in ourselves? Don't we often surprise ourselves with our "hidden" strengths and talents? The wars and personal battles themselves stir within our psyche the sowing of the seeds of recovery and redemption.

In God's covenant with Avraham Avinu[18] the Torah states: "And He said to Avram, 'You shall surely know (*yadoa tedah*) that your seed will be strangers in a land that is not theirs.' "

The midrash[19] expounds on the double use of the words "*yadoa tedah* — you shall surely know" as follows: *yadoa* — "surely know" that I will enslave them (the Jewish people);

tedah — "know" that I will redeem them. The emphasis of the "knowledge" of the slavery *and* redemption of Israel is part of the covenant between God and Avraham. It thus becomes a paradigm, or model, of Jewish history.

The Maharal[20] shows how this model of "ashes to redemption" is a recurring theme of Jewish history. From the furnace of Egypt, God brought us to Har Sinai; from the edict of Haman, we went on to rebuild the Second Temple.[21] That is why the Jewish people mark time by the moon rather than the sun. The moon waxes and wanes, which reflects the triumphs and declines of Jewish history. The midrash[22] states that when Israel is worthy of God's favor it is like the waxing moon, but when it is not worthy, it is compared to the waning moon. That is why during the blessing of *Kiddush Levanah*, the Sanctification of the New Moon, we say: "To the moon He said that it should renew itself as a crown of splendor." Rabbi Joseph B. Soloveitchik states: The Jewish people see in the orderly and lawful motion of the moon in its orbit a process of decline and renewal.[23]

If this model applies to the Jewish nation as a whole, then it also applies to the individual members of the Jewish nation. Many times I have been faced with a seemingly insurmountable crisis, and thank God I have been able to rise above the problem and to steel my character. Through this process God intends for me to learn something, to rectify a certain aspect of my personality,[24] and thereby achieve personal growth. Why does God present these challenges to me? Because He cares for the destiny of my soul and wants me to achieve my potential.

In this first blessing of the *Kerias Shema* — which begins with the *berachah* "*Yotzer Ohr*" (He created light) and ends with *"Yotzer Hame'oros"* (the Creator of the luminaries) — the theme is God as Creator. In addition to the four expressions of praise mentioned above, there are four further expressions in this *berachah* as follows:

5) *Matzmiach yeshuos* — makes salvation flourish,

6) *Borei refuos* — creates cures,

7) *Nora tehillos* — is too awesome for praise,

8) *Adon haniflaos* — is Lord of wonders.

In this *berachah* there are eight expressions, but in reality, states the Iyun Tefillah, there are seven expressions plus an eighth, namely *Adon haniflaos* — an all-embracing praise of God. The seven expressions correspond to the seven days of Creation. There are many applications of the number seven in the Torah and in Halachah, including:

1. Seven-year *shemittah* sabbatical year system — six years working the land; the seventh year the land remains fallow.

2. Seven days of the week — six days of creative interaction with the world; the seventh day is Shabbos, free from creative activity.

3. Seven blessings at the *chuppah* — *Sheva Berachos*.

4. Seven days of sitting *shivah* upon a bereavement.

5. Seven weeks between Pesach and Shavuos.

6. Seven forefathers and foremothers — Avraham, Sarah, Yitzchak, Rivkah, Yaakov, Rachel, and Leah.

7. Seven species of the Land of Israel.

God created the world with a system of "seven" because the world is made up of six physical dimensions and a seventh spiritual dimension. There are six directions in the physical world — north, south, east, west, up, and down. Every physical object in the universe has three dimensions and thus six physical facets or directions. That which sustains the object is the seventh dimension, the spiritual source — God. That is why the seven-day week and the seven-year sabbatical system both end with the "seventh dimension" — freedom. That is why the seventh day of the week is Shabbos — representing the spiritual or soul dimension. Thus, the Maharal states that the number seven represents a complete unit, made up of six physical dimensions and one spiritual dimension.[25]

When I read this first blessing of the *Shema*, the words foster within me a sense of belonging within the created world, which is comprised of these seven dimensions. Just as the world has six physical dimensions and one spiritual source, so, too, do I have six physical dimensions and one God-given life force — my God-given soul. I have a place in this universe because I am created of the same seven dimensions with which the world has been created. I have six dimensions — front, back, two sides, head, and heels — plus a seventh spiritual soul dimension. My being fits into the flow and grain of the universe and thus I belong here; I have a valuable place within God's plan.

The Iyun Tefillah points out that the eighth term in this blessing is *Adon haniflaos* (God is Lord of Wonders), and is a reference to the supernatural power of God. Whereas the number seven is *"sheva"* in Hebrew, which can also be read *"savea,"* meaning full, complete, and satisfied, the number eight or *"shemoneh"* in Hebrew has its roots in the word *"shamen"* — which means "fat," one step beyond my natural state of satisfaction. Thus, not only is God the Creator of the seven basic units of the natural world, He also orchestrates the world from an eighth "supernatural," miraculous dimension, beyond the natural "seven" based system.

There are a number of references to the number eight in the Torah and Halachah:

1. Eight days of Chanukah.

2. Eight vestments of the *kohen gadol*.

3. On the eighth day of its life an animal may be sacrificed.

4. The *Melavah Malka* — the special meal we eat on Saturday night to honor and escort the Sabbath Queen as she departs from our midst on her way into the week. The Saturday night meal is known as the meal of the symbolic "eighth" day of the week, as it is beyond the conclusion of the natural seven-day week. Kabbalists teach that eating the *Melavah Malka* meal spiritually "feeds" the bone at the base of the neck (*luz shebeshidra*) from which the human body will be reformed at *techiyas hameisim*, the revival of the dead in Messianic times.[26]

5. *Bris Milah* — circumcision on the eighth day.

This eighth dimension is the supernatural dimension of the Jewish people. We have enjoyed an "eighth day," i.e., supernatural, relationship with God for over four thousand years. No other nation is still practicing its original way of life as are the Jews. If God has a special close relationship with the nation of Israel, then He must also have an intimate, special, "eighth day" supernatural relationship with each Jew. There is one proviso, however: God will not force Himself on us. If I want to avail myself of this personal relationship with God I am invited to initiate the relationship.

In the midst of this first *berachah* of *Kerias Shema* we find interspersed the *Kedushah* — *Kadosh, Kadosh, Kadosh*[27] and *Baruch Kevod Hashem Mimkomo*.[28] According to Avudraham, the *Kedushah* is inserted here in order to counter the Deist philosophy that God created the world, but then allowed the sun, moon, stars, and nature to run their course without His guidance. Deists suggests that God gave the world a "spin" and has been on vacation ever since. Thus the men of the Great Assembly inserted within this blessing the *Kedushah* — praise of God — which describes the daily orbits of the sun and moon, to emphasize that God is Master of the Hosts of Heaven whose glory fills the earth. This can instill in me the knowledge and realization that God is still involved with the Creation and with me.

In the 1980s there was a hit pop song called "All We Are Is Dust in the Wind." It was a catchy melody and I often found myself moved by the tune, until I paid attention to the lyrics. "All I am is dust in the wind" — I am a meaningless puff of dust particles moved aimlessly by the forces of nature. No wonder lack of self-esteem is such a prevalent problem. Our media-age philosophy promotes and reinforces our uselessness and ultimate worthlessness.

Judaism challenges and has always challenged this idea. I am created *"b'tzelem Elokim,"* in the image of God, and I have a role to play in completing God's creation of the universe, as the Creation story tells us: *"Asher bara Elokim la'asos* — which God created to do." The words "to do," according to Alshich, are God's challenge to me to complete and to perfect the work that He set in motion. If I live my life befitting one who carries within him the "image of God" then I gain a sense of meaning and purpose; I *am* worthwhile to God and important for God's Plan.

The Midrash[29] relates that Tarnusrufus, the Roman Governor of Judea in the first century, challenged Rabbi Akiva and said: "If God is perfect then why did He create man in an imperfect state, being uncircumcised?"

Rabbi Akiva answered by picking up a stalk of wheat and handing it to Tarnusrufus, and said: "Which would you rather eat — this stalk of wheat or bread?"

Tarnusrufus answered: "Bread."

Rabbi Akiva said: "God made the grain and asks man to complete the process of creation by baking it into bread. Thus, man is destined to be a partner with God in Creation. God created an incomplete, imperfect world so that man would be challenged to perfect it."

So, too, it is with *bris milah*. Man is challenged by God to perfect himself by channeling his passions into avenues of *kedushah*.

Now, how does this principle fit in with Rav Elchanan Wasserman's parable quoted earlier whereby God as the Farmer controls the Big Picture as I go through the steps of the baking process? If God guides the overall "wheat to bread" process, then what significant role can I possibly play in perfecting the world? Am I not squeezed out of the process by God's controlling the production process? The answer is that while God sees the Big Picture and guides the overall process, God allows me free will and I am responsible to play my role *within* each stage. Each stage is designed by God with me in mind. I may be given rye, spelt, oats, wheat, or barley. I may be given a fertile field near a stream or an arid field on a mountain. I might live in an area of abundant rain or in drought conditions. I, however, am challenged by God to react to the changing seasons and general conditions by applying my unique insight and ingenuity to the particular set of circumstances that He presents to me. I am therefore involved in an ongoing dynamic relationship with God as I react to the conditions He sets, and He, in turn, changes the weather conditions to respond to my actions and choices.

Each person is given a unique set of circumstances and conditions. Just as our faces are all different, so are our thoughts and abilities.[30] My job is to sow and reap my crop to the best of my abilities at any given point in time. Then I will be doing my share in perfecting myself and the particular field over which I have been given a 120 year leasehold.

Rabbi Boruch HaLevi Epstein asks[31] why this *berachah* ends with the words: *"Hamechadesh b'tuvo b'chol yom tamid ma'aseh bereishis* — Who renews in His Goodness always the Act of Creation,"* since these words are also found right after *Barechu*. He answers that after *Barechu*, the first reference to God as *"Mechadesh"* — Renewer of the world — is a statement without Scriptural authority. Now, at the end of this *berachah* we include the Scriptural source for this concept,[32] as follows: *"L'oseh orim gedolim ki l'olom chasdo* — To Him Who makes the great luminaries, for His kindness endures forever."*

The reason we conclude with a Scriptural verse is to engrave this philosophy in our hearts: it is out of pure kindness that God established the world so that He could bestow His kindness on the world. Mankind, those who can recognize and relate to this kindness, are the "crown of creation" for whom God created the world. Thus, I can be uplifted and encouraged by the fact that God wanted to bestow His kindness on me personally, and that He had me "in mind" when He created the world, to bestow His kindness, His "*ohr*," upon me and within me. Thus, I can hardly be dust in the wind. I am a "*kli*," a receptacle, to receive the kindness, light, and wisdom of God. I can "tap into" that light by studying the wisdom of God — His Torah. As King Solomon states,[33] "*Ki ner mitzvah, v'Torah ohr* — a mitzvah is a candle, and Torah is light.*"

My maternal grandfather, David Abba Hakohen Huberman, *z"l*, relates the following in his book *Kinor David*:

One night, at midnight, Rabbi Yisrael Salanter entered through the gates of a small town whose residents were long asleep. The windows of every house were dark except for the shop window of Reb Yosef, the shoemaker, who sat by the light of a lone candle, repairing the soles of a pair of old shoes. Rabbi Salanter saw the dancing light from the flickering flame, knocked on the window of the shop, and asked to be allowed in.

Once inside, Rabbi Salanter said to the shoemaker: "The flame of your candle is flickering and the light is almost out. Why don't you stop working as the hour is late?"

Reb Yosef replied: "Reb Yisrael, while there remains even the most faint glow from the flame, I still have time to continue my work."

Whilst the soul of man burns within him he can yet learn, grow, and strive for truth; he can still do mitzvos and repair his soul. While Hashem continues to grant him the privilege of life, he can yet develop his character and his *middos*. Only when the soul returns to its Creator is one's work in this world complete. Until then he can and must continue going "*veiter*" (Yiddish for "forward"). As it is written: "The soul of man is the candle of Hashem."[34]

אהבה רבה
Enhancing My Self-Image

A young couple I know consulted me about a problem they were having with their eleven-year-old son. He was an intelligent and sensitive boy, yet somewhere along the line he developed a negative self-image. He felt he was an inadequate student and that he was unliked by his peers. In discussions with his teachers they confirmed that he had academic talent and was popular amongst his friends — yet he held a negative view of himself. No matter how much he succeeded, he felt that he was not "good enough." I recommended that his parents seek out a course of counselling with a child psychologist with expertise in the area of self-esteem enhancement.

During the course of weekly therapy the boy's parents noticed a marked improvement in his attitude and demeanor. He became more self-assured and was carrying himself with more self-confidence. His school work improved. One of the most interesting and telling indicators of his developing positive self-esteem was that his handwriting improved. While he used to write small, almost illegible letters, his forming of the letters grew in stature. The writing in his homework book became much larger, expansive and flowing. The psychologist explained to his parents that since the child was beginning to see himself in a positive light, he began to develop a more positive self-image which was reflected in the "taller" and more expansive formation of the letters in his writing.

This scenario gives us an insight into the words of the second berachah of Kerias Shema:

וְתוֹלִיכֵנוּ קוֹמְמִיּוּת לְאַרְצֵנוּ.

And lead us with upright pride to our land.

The Iyun Tefillah comments that the source of this prayer is in Vayikra,[35] as the Torah states: "And I have broken the bands of your yoke and made you go upright (*komemius*)." Rashi comments: "*Komemius* — [upright] with stature of pride!"

A person may tend to react to a period of personal trauma and crisis by walking with his head down in a slow, shuffling manner. The physical manner and posture of walking is a manifestation of a person's spiritual, emotional, and psychological state. When a person walks with his head held high, a purposeful gait, and a spring in his step — he is displaying an inner attitude of self-worth and positive self-image.

The Midrash states: "The Israelites were mired in the mud and bricks of Egypt, and God extricated them with strength of stature."[36]

The Midrash indicates that the enslavement and torture of the Israelites in Egypt broke their human spirit and dignity. Imagine trying to find meaning and purpose in life if you, your father, and your grandfather had been slaves, and the future prospects are for more of the same. Then God took them out of "*Mitzrayim*" — the narrow "straits" of this degraded self-image — and restored to them their self-esteem as He redeemed them with "His outstretched hand." That is why we say in *Hallel*, "*Min hametzar karasi Kah* — From the narrow straits I called upon Hashem," "*Anani bamerchav Kah* — He answered me with His *merchav*": His broad, all-embracing protection.

The metamorphosis of self-image experienced by the Israelites came about by virtue of their lives taking on renewed
direction, meaning, and purpose when they arrived at Har
Sinai. Thus, the second *berachah* prior to the *Shema* states:

וְקֵרַבְתָּנוּ לְשִׁמְךָ הַגָּדוֹל סֶלָה בֶּאֱמֶת.

*And you brought us close to Your Great Name
forever, in truth.*

The Israelites' change in self-image was not due merely
to their physical freedom from bondage, but more impor-
tantly because they "came close to God's Name," which
means they began to direct and to elevate their lives toward
God's values and standards.

Rabbi Abraham Twerski[37] explains that having purpose
in life is an important component of self-esteem. This second *berachah* of *Kerias Shema* reminds the Jewish people
collectively and each of us individually of our life purpose,
which is to serve *"Shimcha HaGadol — Your Great Name,"*
the Will of God. Each person has a specific and unique portion in bringing himself, herself, our families and friends,
closer to Hashem's "Name," which means His Plan of bringing the world toward its destiny, the perfection of the Messianic Age.

The Talmud states: "A person is obligated to say: 'The
world was created for me.' "[38] This does not mean that the
world must serve my purposes. That would mean that God
was created in *my* image, instead of my having been created
in His image. Rather, in fulfilling my purpose in God's plan,
I will be doing my share to "complete" the world and to
bring the world closer to its perfected state. I can do this by

following the teachings of the Torah to the maximum of my ability. God asks only that given my strengths, talents, and abilities at a given point in time, and taking into account those difficulties which may hamper the full exercise of my capabilities, I am giving it "my best shot." Am I actualizing my potential *at this given moment*?[39] I don't have to achieve someone else's potential — just my own. In this way, I can move the world closer to its potential by actualizing my own.

The Torah states: "Re'eh Anochi nosein lifneichem hayom berachah u'klalah — Behold I place before you today a blessing and a curse."[40] The Kli Yakar asks: Why does the Torah switch from the singular (re'eh) to the plural (lifneichem)? He answers: the Talmud states[41] that a person should always perceive that the world is comprised of one half transgressions and one half merits; if he performs one mitzvah he can shift the balance of his personal scales, and the scales of the entire world, to the side of merits. Therefore, the Torah begins by speaking to each individual: "Re'eh" — See and behold in your mind's eye that your personal actions will come "lifneichem," before the entire community.

Each person's private actions have an obvious impact on his personal scale or equilibrium. I must realize, however, that my actions will also impact upon the energy and equilibrium of the entire world. Yes, "l'il ol'me" can influence and affect the members of my family, my community, and *klal Yisrael*. This realization brings with it a sense of empowerment, but also an awesome responsibility. Since my actions can change the "balance of power" in the spiritual world, then I can allow this realization to improve my perception of my personal value.

שמע ישראל
Coping with Life's Ups and Downs

At times I find it difficult to believe that God really "loves" me. From an intellectual standpoint I know that part of God — my soul — shines within me and that I am therefore "worthy" of God's attention, because there is Godliness within me. However, if He really loved me surely He would make it a little easier for me to navigate the stormy seas of life. Why does He test me with such difficult crises? Why can't He lighten up a bit on me and give me a little break?

The answer lies in the first line of the *Shema*, our declaration of faith: "*Shema Yisrael, Hashem Elokeinu, Hashem Echad* — Hear O Israel, the Lord is our God, the Lord is One." Even though it appears to me as if God is acting toward me with His attribute of justice, alluded to by the name *Elokeinu*, He is really acting toward me with His attribute of mercy, alluded to by the name *Hashem*.

Rabbi Zvi Hirsch Farber,[42] illustrates this concept with the following analogy:

> To what can this be compared? To a doctor who initially allows his patient an unrestricted diet. After a few days, however, the doctor visits the patient and instructs him to observe a strict diet. This does not represent a change in the doctor who is now acting maliciously; rather, this change in diet represents a change in the illness, and this new restrictive diet is prescribed for the wellbeing and recovery of the patient.

Thus, explains Rabbi Farber, this is the meaning of
"Hashem Elokeinu, Hashem Echad — the Lord is our God,
the Lord is One." For *all* of His actions toward me are "One"
— they are all merciful. The change in His prescription, i.e.,
the challenges or crises which He presents to me, are
brought about as a result of a change in my personality, thus
necessitating a different approach from God. He might pre-
scribe a difficult challenge in order to push me to grow and
develop spiritually. He may design a test to address a certain
personality flaw in me so that I can meet the challenge and
rectify the personality defect. Thus, His approach to me may
be a mixture of *Hashem* (mercy) and *Elokeinu* (justice, or a
trying challenge).

I must realize, however, that *"Hashem Echad —* the
Lord is One," that God's purpose is "One" — unified and singular, which is completely merciful, represented by God's
attribute of mercy in His name: *yod-hey-vav-hey.* Even
though on the surface His decree may appear to be harsh, I
must realize that it is all toward "One" purpose — to pro-
mote growth in my personality and bring me closer to perfection, and thus closer to God. Thus, the purpose of God's
presenting me with difficulty is really, in essence, merciful
— it is all "One."

ואהבת את ה׳
Letting Go of Resentment

וְאָהַבְתָּ אֵת ה׳ אֱלֹהֶיךָ בְּכָל לְבָבְךָ, וּבְכָל נַפְשְׁךָ, וּבְכָל מְאֹדֶךָ.

*You shall love the Lord, your God, with all your
heart, with all your soul, and with all your might.*

Even if God acts toward me as *Elokecha* — with His attribute of justice — while He seemingly acts toward others with mercy, I can allow myself to "love God with all my heart" because I know that He is really acting toward me with the ultimate goal of mercy. He merely gets me there through the medium of His attribute of strict justice. Thus, says Rabbi Farber, I can serve God *"b'chol me'odecha"* — which usually means "with all my resources" but which can be read as *"middosecha,"* with all my attributes. This means that with every *middah* with which God interacts with me, I can in turn serve Him "with all my attributes and talents" — with all of my strength and with a full joyous heart. I can love God *"middah keneged middah,"* measure for measure, in response to all the *middos* with which He interacts with me. I can serve Him with a full measure of joy because I know that all of His *middos* are One — of mercy and kindness towards me.

There is one more prerequisite before I can really love Hashem in spite of the seemingly "strict justice" with which He relates to me. Before I can love I have to "let go" of my anger and resentment I feel toward Hashem for presenting me with such a difficult set of personal circumstances. If I know, at least intellectually, that all of Hashem's *middos* toward me are good — then I must muster enough strength to "forgive" Hashem for the tough justice and accept that "this too is for the best." Saying the *Shema* could be that defining moment where I proactively let go of my frustration and consciously place my faith in Hashem. I can elicit this feeling from within me at the moment when I say *"Hashem Echad"* — that Hashem's justice is really One, i.e., kindness. Saying the *Shema* becomes a real act of faith. As the Nesivos Shalom states:[43] When a person performs a mitzvah his heart will be broken within him unless in the midst of doing the mitzvah he feels the presence and closeness of Hashem..." Thus in the midst of saying the *Shema* one must feel the closeness of Hashem by first letting go of the anger...then the way will be clear to begin to love God.

וְהָיוּ לְטטָפֹת בֵּין עֵינֶיךָ.

And they shall be for frontlets between your eyes.

The proper placing of the head tefillin is on top of the head at the point of the fontanelles, where on a baby the skull would be soft and will not yet have grown together. Thus, the tefillin is set behind the eyes at the place on the head which "processes" the images seen by the eyes and sends the impulses to the optic nerve. Thus, the imaging process to analyze the stimuli from the world passes through and is influenced by the spiritual power of the tefillin. In this fashion my "inner eyes" process what I see through a "tefillin perspective." According to Rabbi Zvi Hirsch Farber,[44] my "inner eye" can thus see the outer world from a Jewish perspective.

Halachah, based on the Talmud,[45] states that the term "between your eyes" does not mean between one's eyes above the bridge of the nose on the forehead, rather between the eyes above the hairline. The deeper meaning of this halachic requirement is that I must internalize the message of the tefillin into my internal imaging process — namely, my psyche. My belief and trust in God's "Oneness" and His mercy toward me must remain "in my mind's eye" even after I remove my tefillin. I can imagine I am wearing God's mercy and caring for me "inside" my psyche, which fosters within me an inner balance and an affirming sense of security.

והיה אם שמע
God Invests

וְנָתַתִּי מְטַר אַרְצְכֶם בְּעִתּוֹ.

Then I shall provide rain for your land in its proper time.

Isn't it somewhat religiously primitive to suggest that if I diligently follow Hashem's commandments He will reward me with "rain...in its proper time" — a reference to livelihood? Shouldn't I be "above" this seemingly juvenile form of simple reward and punishment? The Alshich answers that surely the ultimate reward for living a Torah life of heightened spirituality is in the Messianic Age and the World to Come. It is a *chiddush* — an original concept — that the Torah grants us a physical reward in this world rather than "merely" a spiritual one in the next world. The reason we ask for "rain in its proper time" is to smooth the way for us and to make it physically and emotionally easier for us to concentrate on our higher purpose of serving God by following the commandments in this world. Thus, if I ask God for physical reward in this world in order to facilitate my keeping His spiritual commandments, then I am receiving the physical reward as a means to a spiritual end. Far from being a simplified "carrot and stick," this is a high level of "inspired living."[46]

Rain is the embodiment of *berachah* — blessing from God. The Hebrew word for rain is *geshem*, which means "material" or "physical." It forms the root of the word *gashmius*, which means "materialism." Is it too simplistic to think that God provides rain if I ask for it? Certainly not. What I must realize is that God is actually listening to what I have to say. I put my heartfelt case before Him — that I feel I need rain (livelihood) to better fulfill my service of Him. If I have rain, my crops will grow. In modern terms, if I have rain — or livelihood — I can take care of my family, give charity, invite people into my home for Shabbos, and purchase Torah books from which to learn in order to guide my family. If I am using the rains (my livelihood) to further God's purposes, then He will be inclined, God willing, to grant me "rains" in their appointed season.

In order to facilitate my performance of mitzvos in this world, I pray for my physical needs. These physical returns are not *schar* — reward. These are Hashem's investment in my continued service of Him and in my continued personal growth. I must be worthy of this investment by living my life in accordance with God's values and standards. It all comes down to my priorities. Do I live for the physical rewards of this world or for the ultimate spiritual reward in the World to Come? God knows my inner thoughts and desires, for He is *Bochen levavos* — the Tester of hearts. Do I ask God for a successful livelihood so that I can show off my new car, or in order to buy a car to drive my kids to a Jewish school? Am I living to fulfill my short-term needs and desires, or am I asking for my short-term needs in order to help me pursue God's values and standards?

The ultimate reward for our deeds is to be received in the World to Come, as the Talmud states: "There is no reward for a mitzvah in this world."[47]

The Rambam[48] states that a person should return to the

proper Torah path in this world so that when he leaves this world, "he will merit the [true] life in the World to Come."

לְמַעַן יִרְבּוּ יְמֵיכֶם וִימֵי בְנֵיכֶם...

In order to prolong your days and the days of your children...

There are only two commandments in the Torah for which the Torah text indicates the reward for their performance, namely:

1. Honoring parents, which is the fifth of the Ten Commandments,[49] and

2. Shooing away the mother bird. If one comes upon a nest with the mother hovering over her eggs or her young, one shoos away the mother bird and only then takes the eggs or young.[50]

The reward for both of these is "length of days." If this is the case, then why is this general reward of length of days also enumerated in the second paragraph of the *Shema* as a reward for my overall diligent performance of the commandments? I would like to suggest that the meaning here is not so much to grant us "more days" but "breadth" of days, such that each day is lived more fully and meaningfully.

Rabbi Samson Raphael Hirsch, in his Torah commentary on this verse, states that one's "length of days" should be "like the days of the heaven on the earth."[51] Rabbi Hirsch comments that "your days on this earth" are dependent on the "moral blossoming" of your life. If I live my earthly days under the influence of God's heavenly Torah, then this will mirror the natural influence of the heavens over the earth. My position on this earth, and my success in living meaningful earthly days, is dependent on my keeping myself aloft in the heights of my spiritual and moral calling. There is thus an intimate correlation between my spiritual or "heavenly" behavior and my physical or earthly sustenance.

At the end of a person's life, he or she will invariably look back and lament the wasted "down time" he or she experienced in life. "If only I would have taken fuller advantage of life," one might say. "I wish I could have a few more days or minutes, and I would live to the full." As Queen Anne of England said on her deathbed, "All my possessions...for a little more time."

One of the most compelling thoughts that I had when I was considering leaving my law practice, to take off some time to learn in yeshivah, was the regret I would have experienced at the end of my life had I not added this experience to my life's adventure. I thereby projected myself into my "future" senior years and turned to my projected "elderly" wife, and said: "Remember that time that we had the chance to go and study in Israel? I wish we had had the guts to do it. If only we had had the courage." With these thoughts in mind, I transported myself back to the present, told my senior partner I was leaving, and we packed our bags in preparation for the experience of studying in yeshivah in Jerusalem. Those days will always be with me as life-enhancing "breadth of days."

ויאמר ה׳ אל משה
The "I" of the Matter

וְלֹא תָתוּרוּ אַחֲרֵי לְבַבְכֶם וְאַחֲרֵי עֵינֵיכֶם.

*You shall not stray after your heart and after
your eyes.*

It sometimes happens that when I am progressing toward a goal in my studies or on a project, and I come within
striking distance of success, my "eye" catches sight of some
type of distraction and I get thrown off track. That is exactly
what this verse of the *Shema* is saying: "Do not stray after
your eyes." As Rashi tells us: "The eye sees and the heart desires and the limbs perform [the transgression]."[52] It seems
that the "eyes" have it.

Not so fast. Rav Dessler states that my eyes only look
where my internal voice tells me to look.[53] My eyes are only
distracted because my mind's eye, i.e., my inner inclination,
desired that thing and thus guided me to look for such a distraction. If only I could "get in touch" with and control my
inner inclination, my *"ratzon"* or "inner will," then I could
stay on track and see my project through to its proper conclusion.

With this thought we come to the "eye" or "I" of the matter. What does the real inner "I" desire? Whatever I desire or
"will" is in essence the real me. If I could only delve into my
nekudah hapenimis, my central core and essence, I could
find out who I am and get to know my real self. This would
be a moment of personal clarity, enlightenment,
self-knowledge, and self-awareness. I could get in touch
with my "internal" desire at will and activate my
self-concept by working on activating and building up my
self-esteem. How do I achieve this?

וַעֲשִׂיתֶם אֶת כָּל מִצְוֹתָי וִהְיִיתֶם קְדֹשִׁים לֵאלֹהֵיכֶם.

And perform all My commandments, and be holy to your God.

God is *Kadosh* — holy — which means He is beyond the physical limits of this world. If I could "tap in" to God's "*kedushah*" — the spark of holiness, that pristine perfection that Hashem planted within me — then I could push the button of my "inner core." If I could close my eyes and dig deep into my inner being and locate some point within me of inner goodness, inner warmth, and inner light, I would be reaching my inner core. I would then draw an imaginary line from that inner point to the source of that *kedushah*, Hashem, and I will have thus activated the "fuel line" to allow Hashem to pour more of His *kedushah* into my inner being.

Rabbi Abraham Twerski, in his book *I am I*,[54] states that without a personal relationship with God there can be no self-esteem. If I realize that my *kedushah*, my inner sanctity, my innate goodness, has been given to me by the Source of Perfection, then I can begin to feel an inner sense of worth and value. I must learn to allow myself to "tap into" the treasure house of *kedushah* and ask Hashem to increase the flow of goodness into my being so that the spark of inner goodness within me can grow into an ember, and then into a flame. In this way I can cause my self-concept to crystallize.

אֲנִי ה' אֱלֹהֵיכֶם אֲשֶׁר הוֹצֵאתִי אֶתְכֶם מֵאֶרֶץ מִצְרַיִם לִהְיוֹת לָכֶם לֵאלֹהִים.

I am the Lord your God, Who has taken you out of the land of Egypt to be for you a God.

Sometimes I find myself in an *"Eretz Mizrayim"* (Straits of Egypt) mood. Things are going well, I have completed a project, and I feel on top of the world. This is an *"Eretz Mizrayim"* mood because the essence of Mizrayim is "self-sufficiency." The mainstay of Egyptian life, economy, and theology was the Nile River. It was their sustainer, water supply, and irrigation source. The problem was — it was always there. The Egyptian did not rely on rain. He was self-sufficient; he just went down to the Nile and it always provided for his needs. Egypt is *"Mizrayim"* — which literally means "narrow," because she embodied a narrow, self-sufficient world view. The Nile was Egypt — and the Nile was her god. The Almighty in His mercy took the Israelites out of Mizrayim — out of this philosophy of self-sufficiency — *"l'hios lachem l'Elokim,"* to be for you a God, so that they would be able to pray to God and to rely upon Him.[55] The Land of Israel does not have a Nile — she relies on rainfall for her sustenance.[56] The nation of Israel is privileged not to be self-sufficient but to be wholly reliant on the beneficence of the Almighty.[57]

When I was living in Jerusalem in 1990, there had been no rainfall well into December, the usual rainy season. The country is agricultural, dependant on rainfall. The *roshei yeshivah* decreed that all *b'nei yeshivah* (seminary students) should insert a special prayer for rain in their daily prayers. Eventually, the cumulative prayers of the nation reached the Almighty and the rains came.

A member of my shul told me that he inserted a special prayer for the recovery of a friend in the *"Refaenu"* (healing) prayer of the *Shemoneh Esrei*, and yet his friend's condition had not improved. I pointed out that just because God did not improve his friend's condition did not mean that God was rejecting his prayers. "Maybe God needs you to feel close enough to Him to ask Him with more intensity and passion," I said. For example, when Israeli soldier Nachshon Waxman, *z"l*, was kidnapped and held by terrorists, Jews around the world prayed that his life be spared. Israeli commandos stormed the house where he was being held, but he was tragically murdered. An Israeli reporter asked Nachshon's father why the prayers of so many were not answered. At the *shivah* for his son some of the commandos who tried to rescue Nachshon came to be *menachem avel* and told the Wachsman family that there was such an intense battle when they stormed the site that it was a miracle that any of the commandos survived. Nachshon's father then said: "God did answer their prayers. They were heard by God, and He spared the lives of many Jewish boys. Only my son was not one of them." Sometimes we pray for something, and God counts it somewhere else.

The Talmud[58] tells us that Hashem sometimes sends us difficulties because "the Almighty desires the prayers of the righteous." God certainly does not need my praises and prayers; He is already perfect. His will is that I fulfill my purpose in life by coming closer to Him. One of the ways I come closer to God is through prayer. Hashem often decides that sometimes it is better for my personal growth for me to plead to God for someone's recovery or for a certain benefit so that I can grow spiritually by realizing how reliant I am on Him. God desires my coming closer to Him not for His sake, but for mine.[59] The more I pray to God with passion, need, and reliance, the more I am making God into *"lachem L'Elokim* — for you a God," and I thus come closer to fulfilling the purpose of my existence.

אמת ויציב ונכון
Thinking Straight

I have a confession to make. In the midst of all of the constant pressures and stresses that act upon me, and due to the myriad short-term and long-term issues that are "on my plate," I might sometimes react to the turmoil by "losing my grip." If I stop to contemplate all of the responsibilities and obligations, as well as the demands on my time and attention, I can momentarily find myself in "confusion mode." I say to myself: Where am I? What do I have to do next? How can one person deal with all this? I may momentarily lose my bearings and my "grip" on the steering wheel of life.

How do I come out of such a mode?

Sometimes I can talk myself out of it. If I realize that the confusion is merely caused by the *yetzer hara* doing his job, then I can step back and look at the confusion mode in perspective. I tell myself: I know exactly where I am. I have to focus on my next task and responsibility. I *can* deal with all this; Hashem is presenting these issues to me, so obviously He knows I can work through these issues and grow spiritually through the experience. If I just focus on one problem at a time and compartmentalize them, I can deal with each problem in its turn. After all, "for everything there is a season."[60]

אַתָּה הוּא רִאשׁוֹן וְאַתָּה הוּא אַחֲרוֹן...

You are the First and You are the Last...

It is the job of the *yetzer hara* to throw me off stride and to make me think that I must deal with all of my problems at once. I then feel overwhelmed and "lose my grip." I try to regain my grip by saying to myself: "Who is in charge here?" The answer: Hashem — "There is no one like Him."[61] He is the *Rishon* (First) and He is the *Acharon* (Last). Even though the *yetzer hara* wants to confuse me by making me believe that "I am lost," I can regain my bearings by focusing on the fact that there is a plan and that God is the *Rishon* and *Acharon* — the First and the Last. He devised the Plan for the universe and He placed me into the world to play my role in the Plan — and I am on track.

The Metzudas Dovid explains the verse[62] upon which this part of *shacharis* is based, as follows: "*Ani Rishon v'Ani Acharon* — I am the First and I am the Last." *Ani Rishon* — I am the First...when? Before the creation of the universe. *V'Ani Acharon* — I am the Last...Who will still be there after the universe is completed.

If I realize that God is in control and experience the feeling of security in His guiding of my life, I can then regain my stride and get back on track.

There is a second thinking process that can help me out of "confusion mode." The Etz Yosef explains the verse "You are the First and You are the Last" as follows:

> *Atah Hu Rishon* — You are the first, You wrought miracles and wonders for us during the redemption process from Egyptian slavery, our first exile and our first redemption. Thus, Hashem is the First because he put us in and pulled us through our first exile. *V'Atah Hu Acharon* — You are the last, to show us miracles and wonders in this exile, which

is our last exile and will lead us to our final redemption.

Hashem is the *last* because He is here with us in exile, as the Torah states: *"V'shav Hashem Elokecha es shevus'cha —* And the Lord your God will return your exile...."[63]

Rashi comments as follows: "It should have said: 'And He caused your exiles to return.' From here we learn that metaphorically the *Shechinah* dwells with Israel in the pain of her exile." This means that God is the Last — He is the Bottom Line and He is with us during this last exile and will return with us from this exile.

God delivered us from Egypt, our original exile. This original exile is the model of Jewish history: exile to redemption, ashes to rebirth. The four subsequent exiles follow the same pattern:

1. Babylonian exile. After the destruction of the First Temple we were exiled by Nebuchadnetzar to Babylon.

2. Persian exile. After Persia conquered Babylon we were subjugated by Persia. After the Purim story we returned to Israel to rebuild the Second Temple, seventy years after the destruction of the First Temple.

3. Greek exile. After the Greeks conquered the Persian Empire and Israel, we were under Hellenistic rule for 180 years. The light of Chanukah prevailed against the darkness of Hellenism, and we emerged from this exile with our religious and political sovereignty represented by the rededication of the Temple.

4. Roman exile. Following the destruction of the Second Temple in 70 C.E., the Romans were God's agents, as

the Torah states: "God will scatter you among all the people, from the end of the earth to the end of the earth."[64] We are now in the midst of this last and longest exile. Yet our faith is still practiced and Jews around the world are returning to Torah-true Judaism in greater numbers than ever before in Jewish history. There are more people learning in yeshivos than at anytime in the last 1500 years. We can feel God's presence with us in the midst of this last exile, as the Torah states: "Hashem — it is He who goes before you; He will be with you; He will not release you nor will He forsake you; do not be afraid and do not be dismayed."[65]

God has a track record. From Egyptian, Babylonian, Persian, and Greek hands He delivered us. We are still practicing our faith during this fourth and final Roman (Western) exile. God has earned our trust in Him. Despite bleak periods of Jewish history, God has "been there" for His people and has redeemed us as a people. *"Am Yisrael Chai* — the Nation of Israel lives."

A nation is made up of individuals. If God "is there" for the nation He is also there for the individuals who comprise that nation. I have experienced periods of personal exile when I have felt I was "alone against the world." Yet, God was there with me in the midst of my personal isolation and despair. He has redeemed me from my personal exiles and He can pull me through my current mini-exile of being in "confusion mode." I may have momentarily "lost my grip" but I must remember that *"Atah Hu Rishon, v'Atah Hu Acharon"* — You were there for me in my first exile and You are with me in this, my last, most recent exile.

What I must remember is that there is a *beginning* and a

purpose to my life's journey. There is a goal and a process of beginning to end. Even though I may have been temporarily thrown off the course of my journey, I can get back on track. I must realize that there is a process that God is guiding me through and that I *must* be going through in order to achieve my next level of character and personal development. If I put my momentary "confusion mode" into the perspective of my process of "exile to redemption," then I can allow myself an opportunity to regain my footing, get my train back on track, and continue my personal journey toward my next station in life.

NOTES

1. *Berachos* 11b.
2. *Bereishis Rabbah*, ch. 9.
3. Bereishis 1:31.
4. *Reb Elchanan — The Life and Times of Rabbi Elchanan Wasserman* (New York: Mesorah Publications, Ltd., 1982), 411–412.
5. *Nefesh HaChaim, sha'ar alef*, ch. 2.
6. An angel in Hebrew is a *malach*, which means "messenger." God uses the natural forces, i.e., gravity, the weak and strong forces, photosynthesis, and all other biological and teleological systems, to act as His messengers in running the world.
7. Keleman, *Permission to Believe*, p. 51.
8. Rabbi Uziel Milevsky, *z"l*, Ohr Somayach Yeshivah, Jerusalem, 1990.
9. *Chovos HaLevavos, Sha'ar HaYichud*, chs. 6 and 7.
10. Bereishis 1:14.
11. The halachic requirement to daven the *shacharis Amidah* begins at *neitz* and continues for four relative hours (one third of the day).
12. The halachic time to daven *minchah Amidah* is thirty minutes after midday and continues until sunset.
13. Chofetz Chaim, *Shem Olam, chelek sheni*, ch. 10.
14. Yeshayahu 22:13.

15. Rabbi Yehudah Silver, London, 1993.

16. *Berachos* 60b.

17. *Nefesh HaChaim, sha'ar alef,* ch. 2.

18. Bereishis 15:13–14.

19. *Bereishis Rabbah* 44:19.

20. *Netzach Yisrael.*

21. Joseph B. Soloveitchik, *Halachic Man* (Philadelphia: Jewish Publication Society of America, 1983), 106.

22. *Shemos Rabbah* 15.

23. The ultimate renewal of the moon to "be as the light of the sun" (Yeshayahu 30:26) is a prayer for the ultimate redemption of the waning moon, which is representative of the ultimate redemption of the Jewish people.

24. This concept of rectification, or *tikun,* means that I have an opportunity to rectify past mistakes that I may have made in a previous incarnation. See the concept of *tikun nefesh,* rectification of the soul, in *Sha'ar Hagilgulim,* Arizal.

25. *Tiferes Yisrael,* ch. 2.

26. *Bereishis Rabbah* 28:3.

27. Yeshayahu 1:3.

28. Yechezkel 3:12.

29. *Midrash Tanchuma, parashas Tazria.*

30. *Bamidbar Rabbah* 21:2.

31. *Baruch She'amar.*

32. Tehillim 136:7.

33. Mishlei 6:25.

34. Ibid. 20:27.

35. 26:13.

36. *Shemos Rabbah,* ch. 25.

37. Abraham Twerski, *Let Us Make Man* (New York: CIS Publishers, 1989), 109–117.

38. *Sanhedrin* 37a.

39. Twerski, *Let Us Make Man,* p. 115.

40. Devarim 11:26.

41. *Kiddushin* 40b.

42. *Siach Tzvi, Shema Yisrael.*

43. In his essay, "*V'hinei Hashem Nitzav Alav,*" parashas Vayeitzei.

44. *Siach Tzvi, U'letotafos bein Einecha.*

45. *Menachos* 37b.
46. The title of a book written by Rabbi Akiva Tatz is *Living Inspired* (Jerusalem: Targum Press, Inc., 1993).
47. *Kiddushin* 39b.
48. *Hilchos Teshuvah* 7:1.
49. Shemos 20:12.
50. Devarim 22:67.
51. Ibid. 11:21.
52. Bamidbar 15:39.
53. *Michtav MiEliyahu*, "Mabat HaEmet," vol. 1, pp. 52–57.
54. P. 21.
55. Rabbi Moshe Shapiro, Jerusalem.
56. Devarim 11:11–12 states: "But the land to which you cross over to possess is a land of hills and valleys, from the rain of Heaven will it drink water; a land that Hashem, your God, seeks out; the eyes of Hashem, your God, are always upon it from the beginning of the year to year's end."
57. *Ta'anis* 11a.
58. *Yevamos* 64a.
59. The *Maharsha* comments that when I pray, I acknowledge that Hashem has the power to grant my request. I become more humble and thus change my nature from one who is self-sufficient to one who is more reliant on God. Therefore, I now deserve more favorable treatment from God.
60. Koheles 3:3.
61. Devarim 4:35.
62. Yeshayahu 44:6.
63. Devarim 30:3.
64. Ibid. 28:64.
65. Ibid. 31:8.

Chapter 4

THE AMIDAH

שמונה עשרה
The Inner Self

While the term *"tefillah"* does generally mean prayer, in halachic terms it refers to one prayer in particular, namely the *Shemoneh Esrei* — the nineteen blessings also known as the *Amidah*, the Standing Prayer, or the Silent Devotion. The Talmud tells us that the *Chasidim Rishonim* (a select group of Sages) used to spend one hour in reflection preparing for *tefillah*, one hour in prayer itself, and one hour in denouement following prayer.[1] This leads us to the conclusion that this central and pivotal *tefillah* was an intense period of connection and closeness to God. In fact it can be a personal journey into the *deeper levels of self and consciousness* — a quasi self-introspective meditation. The *Amidah*, which is usually said in many of our shuls in under three minutes, is a most under-utilized prayer. If I would be able to understand the depth and the power of the *Amidah* connection to my Creator, I would experience a few moments of introspective self-analysis — and thereby personal renaissance.

The *Amidah* opens with establishing my *yichus* or "lineage credentials" as a descendant of our forefathers Avraham, Yitzchak, and Yaakov. Yaakov earned an additional name, Yisrael, after he wrestled with the angel prior to his encounter with his brother Esav. Why then, asks Rabbi Zvi Hirsh Farber,[2] is Yaakov not known in the *Amidah* as Yisrael? Rabbi Farber answers that when Yaakov prayed to God after Yisrael was added to his name, the Torah states: "Then Yaakov said: 'God of my father Avraham, and God of my father Yitzchak, Hashem, Who said to me, "Return to your Land..." ' "[3]

When Yaakov poured out his heart in prayer to God, beseeching God's protection and pleading that he be seen worthy of it, he is referred to as Yaakov rather than Yisrael. Rabbi Farber explains that since he is referred to as Yaakov when he was about to encounter Esav, who appeared to be coming toward him with an army to kill him for having "stolen" Esav's birthright, he is thus referred to in the *Amidah* as Yaakov. There is a profound insight in this explanation. We mentioned earlier that a person's name, or *shem*, is a reflection of their *neshamah*, or life force. When Yaakov brought his life force face to face with God as he prayed for his life, he was facing God as the Ultimate Reality of the universe. Since he was pleading that his life be given the opportunity to continue playing its role in God's plan, he put his life into God's hands.

This is the feeling that I should strive for each time I stand in Silent Devotion before God. I should feel as if my life is "on the line" and that I am pleading that I be given the chance to fulfill my life's destiny. When I place my "life force" into intense conversation with God, I want to tap into the same spiritual frequency that Yaakov initiated.

When I pray I am causing my unique essence, my *neshamah* or life force, to come face to face with its Source. This is a "close encounter of the real kind." When I place my yearnings and inner desires before my Source, Hashem, it can be a moment of great emotional and spiritual closeness to God, called *kirvas Elokus*. I feel vulnerable by opening up my *nekudah hapenimis*, my "inner core," to God, yet at the same time I feel that warm closeness of God's embrace as I reveal to Him my deepest feelings, fears, hopes, and dreams. More than merely presenting God with a shopping list of petitions and requests, I place my desire for meaning and direction into the outstretched arms of the Almighty. This is the moment that my real self, my *ratzon*, meets His *Ratzon*, His Will for me. In this moment my authentic "name," my God-given name or essence, comes "face to face" with God. This is the Yaakov in me — my original essence meets its Origin.

When Yaakov was awarded the extra name "Yisrael" it was an addition that Yaakov earned. He took the Yaakov in him — the original character and personality that God gave him at birth — and earned an additional and higher spiritual level — Yisrael. As the Torah states: "You have striven with God and with men, and you prevailed."[4]

When Yaakov presented his original "self" to God, he worked on his inner personality and added a new dimension called — "Yisrael." When I pray to God in the *Shemoneh Esrei*, I bring my original, authentic self before the throne of Glory, and I thus engage in a *cheshbon hanefesh*, a searching moral inventory. The term *"l'hispalel,"* to judge, is in the reflexive form, meaning "to judge oneself." I need this process of self-judgment in order to assess whether I will truly serve Hashem better with the resources that I am requesting in this particular prayer. Only if I engage in an honest self-appraisal can I truly come to know myself — my strengths and my weaknesses. My life's goal is to work on and to wrestle with my God-given "Yaakov" self and to develop my attributes, values, and personality and thereby augment it with the dimension of "Yisrael" — which means to reveal the *yashar-El*,[5] the truth of God's standard. If I build upon and broaden my "Yaakov" self, adding the aspect of "Yisrael" through personal effort, and by striving to improve myself by acting more Godly, then I will surely reveal more of the greatness of God's standards and values in the world.[6] I can only achieve my unique mission and purpose in creation if I bring my Yaakov to God and ask for His assistance in maturing my natural self into my earned self[7] — my Yisrael.

אתה חונן
Decisions, Decisions

I used to find it difficult to make decisions. When I was in the midst of the process of deciding which university to attend, I convinced myself that Brandeis University was the place for me. The next day I was convinced Yeshiva University was the place to be. In fact, I remember changing my mind nine times in the course of a single thirty-minute bus journey from my high school to my home. I eventually decided on Yeshiva University.

While practicing law, I was actively involved in Jewish community work, including coordinating weekend seminars for NCSY (National Conference of Synagogue Youth), organizing one-to-one study centers, and teaching Talmud to various students. I found myself gaining a tremendous amount of personal satisfaction from my community involvement, and I began contemplating taking some time off to pursue my life-long dream of becoming a rabbi.

I agonized during the decision-making process, which took approximately three years. A career change was a major life decision, and I wanted to make an informed decision in the best interests of my family. One afternoon at my law firm, the lawyers and legal secretaries were discussing what they would do if they won the lottery. One said he would travel, another said she would buy a country cottage. I said I would take time off and become a rabbi. Charles Markowitz, the senior partner of my firm, turned to me and said, "If you really wanted to become a rabbi, then money would be no object. If it really is your dream, then you should do it."

His comment made me realize that I had something very precious. It revealed to me one of the keys to the decision-making process. He empowered me to resolve my dilemma by pointing out one crucial fact: subject to certain life circumstances, I can point myself toward my own destiny despite challenges like financial considerations. If I really wanted this, I could find a way. This realization allowed me to release myself from the chains of indecision. It revealed to me a method of resolving the internal anguish and turmoil of inner conflict: namely, that in many cases, I have the power, through my God-given free will, to plan and to take charge of my own life. This, of course, does not alone guarantee the success of my choices or that I will arrive at what I think is my destination of choice. After some further deliberation, my wife and I decided to take some time off to study in Israel.

This fourth blessing of the *Amidah* — which is the first of thirteen *bakashos*, petitions — requests wisdom and insight. It is akin to my senior partner making me focus on the fact that God has given me understanding and insight in order to exercise my God-given free choice, called *"bechirah chofshis"* — free will. God is my Senior Partner, and He empowers me every day with the knowledge and wisdom to help me clarify the issues, pros, and cons which will allow me, in turn, to make an informed choice.

"Atah chonen l'adam da'as — You graciously endow man with wisdom...." The Chofetz Chaim, Rabbi Yisroel Meir Kagan, states:

> One must concentrate and consciously understand this *berachah*, because this is the main request that man must make of the Creator: that He grant him the power of clear discernment and wisdom to reject evil and to choose the good.[8]

The *Shulchan Aruch* teaches us that a man is elevated above the animal by virtue of the power of discernment. While an animal acts on pre-programmed instinct and impulse, I on the other hand must check my instincts and ask myself whether acting upon a particular instinct or impulse is beneficial for my spiritual essence — my soul. God has confidence in me that I can follow His instructions as to how to draw close to Him. It is liberating and inspiring to realize that the Creator actually "believes" in me. This gives me a sense of inner strength and self-confidence in that God values me and my ability to choose my own pathway within the framework that He has given me — the Torah.

Let us now pose a question. Just because God has confidence in my power to choose, that may be merely symptomatic of a general confidence God has in mankind, rather than His trust in me, personally. Why does it follow that God granting mankind free will can instill in *me*, personally, an inner value and self-worth which is the foundation of self-esteem? The Kuzari, Rabbi Yehudah Halevi, states: "Man is always positioned between two alternatives, and he has the option to choose whichever one he desires. He is therefore either praised or condemned, depending on his choice."[9]

If I delve deeply into my psyche and try to locate the place from which my decisions emanate — then I can put my finger on my soul. This self-awareness is a prerequisite for self-esteem. Once I realize that I have a God-given decision-making center, then I can realize that each person's genetic and environmental make-up is unique, thus creating the scenario for a unique decision to be made by each individual, including me.

No wonder it is difficult to make decisions. We are put in this world precisely to make decisions. I am, in essence, a "bundle of choices." This is my *raison d'etre* — my reason for being: to choose to order my life in such a way as to come close to the Source of all decision making power (God). When I exercise my unique free will, I work towards achieving my unique potential, and if I can choose correctly I can then make that unique contribution for which I was placed into this world.

The Ibn Ezra wonders how Moshe, having learned the supreme wisdom of the Torah on Mount Sinai, could possibly comprehend the vast secrets of the Torah such that they would be contracted into the physical state of Ten Commandments written on two tablets of stone. To answer this question, the Ibn Ezra quotes Yirmiyahu as follows: "But let him that glories, glory in this: that he understand and know Me."[10]

The Ibn Ezra continues: "It is not possible to know God unless one knows his own spirit, soul, and body. Anyone who does not know the nature of his own spirit — what knowledge can he attain?"

The Ibn Ezra seems to be saying that a prerequisite to entering into a relationship with God is to get to know myself — or to have a relationship with my "self."

I must realize that while I can never come to understand the nature or essence of God's wisdom, I could not possibly embark upon or enter into a relationship with Him unless there was something of value in me to which God could, in His terms, relate. God established within me the capacity to contemplate the wonders of life and my own Source. The more I stand in awe of my own wondrous symmetrical body, the beauty of nature, and appreciation for the spiritual, the more I will come to know myself — and the "*gadlus ha'adam*," the greatness of man that God created in me. Rabbeinu Yonah in the opening words of *Sha'arei Teshuvah* states: "The first principle is that a person who is a servant of God should know his own value and self-worth and that he should recognize his own greatness and the greatness of his ancestors."

השיבנו אבינו
The Root Soul

My ancestor, Rabbi Yisroel Charif of Satanov, states[11] that the concept of *"Avinu,"* our Father, is a reference to the Source — "the beginning" — when I say: *"Hashiveinu, Avinu, l'Sorasecha* — Bring us back, our Father, to your Torah."

When I begin to observe a Torah way of life, I return to the original spark of Torah in my soul which God Himself planted within me. The Iyun Tefillah quotes the beautiful Talmudic statement[12] that a fetus in its mother's womb studies the entire Torah from the mouth of an angel. At the moment of birth the angel touches the child on the upper lip, causing the baby to forget all of its Torah knowledge. Thus I pray that God help me return to the Torah that I learned in the womb. This seemingly quaint midrash has a profound message. The fetus learns Torah because the Torah is encoded in the spiritual genes of the fetus. This means that the Torah's wisdom, which is the expression of God's will, comprises the spiritual DNA of my very chromosomes. When a person is inspired to become a *"ba'al teshuvah"* (a person who "returns" to a Torah-observant way of life), he or she is not blazing a new trail. He or she is returning home to his or her *"pintelle yid"* — the Jewish spark which is already burning within his or her inner being.

When a person gains an insight or a new idea it is often depicted in cartoons as a lightbulb being turned on over his head. This lightbulb implies that the idea or knowledge already existed within the person's psyche, and that a stimulus sparked the information center deep within the recesses of his psyche; then he "shed light" or illuminated the closet of his inner mind, which revealed this "new" (already present) idea.[13] The same principle applies to *teshuvah* — the wellspring of Torah is already there. I must only return to it and be revived by its waters.

No matter how far a person strays from Jewish practice and observance, explains the Etz Yosef, he can still "return" at any time because of his spiritual inheritance, as the Torah states: *"Torah tzivah lanu Moshe, morashah kehillas Yaakov* — the Torah that Moses commanded us is the heritage of the Congregation of Yaakov."[14]

The son of a king does not lose his inheritance if he is on a worldwide tour and is away from his father for some time. Thus I pray for God's spiritual guidance to inspire me to claim that which is rightfully mine — my unique inheritance in the Torah of Israel.

The "Judaic spark" of Torah DNA was planted within our souls at Mount Sinai, as the Torah states: "With whoever is here, standing with us today before Hashem, our God, and with whoever is not here with us today."[15] Rashi comments as follows: "...and even with the generations which were yet to come."

This means that all future generations would be bound by the covenant entered into by the original Jewish nation at Mount Sinai. Thus, even though I live today 3300 years after the giving of the Torah on Mount Sinai, I am *"Nishba v'omed meHar Sinai* — Sworn to keep the Torah since Mount Sinai"[16] and therefore obligated to keep the Torah. When a nation's government enters into a treaty, it binds future generations of citizens to adhere to that treaty even though those future generations did not sign the original agreement. So, too, the Jewish nation entered into the original covenant at

Sinai which binds all future generations of citizens of the Jewish nation — as part of the ongoing national entity called *Am Yisrael*.

Thus, this *berachah* of the *Amidah* states: "Influence us to return in perfect repentance before You."

These words refer to my journey back to my root soul which was imprinted with Torah DNA on Mount Sinai. This is why the *ba'al teshuvah* feels fulfilled and *"shalem,"* whole and contented, because his/her way of life is now on track with its original mission to serve God which it accepted on Mount Sinai. It is a feeling described by many newly observant Jews as "it feels right" — "it fits" — "it brings my life together."

There are those who translate the Hebrew term *"teshuvah"* as "repentance." This brings to mind "fire and brimstone," thunderbolts, and fleeing from a little red man with a pitchfork. Nothing could be further from the truth. The proper translation of the term *"teshuvah"* is "return." It means a return to God and the way of life that He has bestowed upon us — the Torah way of life.

Rabbi Shlomo Rokeach of Belz said that there are three types of exile: First, there is the Jew's exile among the nations; second, a Jew's exile among his fellow Jews when he feels alienated from them; and third, a Jew when he feels alien to his own self. *Teshuvah* means coming home "to myself"; getting my priorities straight and fulfilling the task and mission that God has designed especially for me. When I get to know my *"nekudah hapenimis"* — my inner core — I can begin to feel inner peace.

Rabbi Mayer Schiller[17] asks: How can you return to a place you have never been? He answers: You have been there. You once did shake hands with God on Mount Sinai 3300 years ago. *Teshuvah* means coming back home to re-experience how you felt when you stood at the foot of Mount Sinai with three million other Jews and witnessed God giving the Torah to Moshe.

The last words of this *berachah* of the *Amidah* express the most important concept of *teshuvah:* "Blessed is God, Who wants my return."

You mean God will not allow my past misdeeds to stand in the way of my return to a Torah way of life? He won't turn me away even if I have been somewhat "adventurous" in my life? You mean He "accepts" my return? You mean He actually knows when I return and wants "me" to return to Him? Little, insignificant me? Yes. I am not insignificant. If God wants my return, my service, and my growth, then I feel a deep sense of security as I place myself in God's hands. I feel His warm encouraging embrace. He holds me close to His essence and wipes my tears from my face. He says, "Welcome back, my child."

סלח לנו
Self-Motivation

After I have "returned" to God by changing my attitude and begin to engage God in a relationship by living His Torah, then I can spell out my individual mistakes, and go through a "mini Yom Kippur confession." Yom Kippur is not a "downer," rather, it is highly uplifting and inspiring. It is the day that commemorates God's forgiving of the Jewish people for the sin of the Golden Calf. He displayed His forgiveness by giving the Jewish people the second set of Ten Commandments, which were brought by

Moshe to the Jewish people on Yom Kippur. Yom Kippur is actually a day which commemorates our second receiving of the Torah. Thus Yom Kippur is a joyous occasion of closeness between God and the Jewish people. Yom Kippur, then, should not be seen as an awful day — but a day of awe.

God imprinted this day for all time with His forgiveness. When we annually enter into this "time zone" of Yom Kippur we re-enter a spiritual zone which is saturated with God's closeness and forgiveness. Time moves in a spiral rather than linearly.[18] Therefore, every time I enter a "time zone" of another holiday, i.e., Yom Kippur, Pesach, Shavuos, and perform its mitzvos and rituals, I can actually feel the spiritual energy that the Israelites experienced when they originally celebrated that particular event or holiday in Jewish history. The mitzvos and rituals of the holiday are the computer cables which allow my *neshamah* to access the spirituality of my ancestors. The mitzvos are the web site address which allows me entry into the web page of Jewish spirituality.

On Yom Kippur I hit my chest with my right hand in confession for the mistakes I made during the year. This does not make Judaism into a masochistic, self-flagellating tribe of superstitious ancients. I hit my chest because I have the courage to take personal responsibility for my errors. I hit my heart and say to it: *"Atah garamta li* — You caused me to err."

I hit my heart, as it is the heart that is my "desire center" which caused me to swerve from the path that my *neshamah* would have liked me to follow. I hit my heart and say: I can be a better son, daughter, father, mother, employee, servant of God. I hit my heart, not to knock myself down, but to motivate and to inspire myself to grow in areas of my personality in which I may have sold myself short. Yom Kippur is thus a day of personal self-reflection and "fearless inventory" to cause me to contemplate my personal growth.[19]

The moment I am willing to take responsibility for my mistakes and redirect myself is a moment of great spiritual empowerment. Yom Kippur celebrates my ability to take charge of my life. This thought pattern can serve to strengthen my self-worth and value in that on this day I realize that I can develop my personality. This moment of realization is empowering to my psyche and to my self-esteem.

One of the most important things I learned at parenting school is never to call my child "a bad boy" or a "naughty girl." Rather, I must differentiate between the child himself or herself and the actions of the child. The act of the child was not appropriate — but the child must be validated. For example, I might say: "I love you, my child, but I am disappointed in what you just did. You are capable of much better behavior. I have confidence in you that you can improve your behavior." In this way I maintain the child's positive self-perception as a person of value while trying to encourage the child to improve his or her behavior.

This model can apply to my own self-perception as I enumerate my mistakes during this *berachah* of *Selach lanu Avinu* — "Forgive us, our Father." I must be able to differentiate between my person and my actions. While my actions may have been inappropriate, I am still a person of value. This is implied in the words "Forgive us, our Father": Forgive me, Hashem, even though "I" — my soul, my essence — chose to exercise its free will inappropriately. The essence of

my soul is my *ratzon* or will. At my core is my decision-making headquarters — centered in my soul. The "I" in
me is identified with my "choosing center."

Even if I choose incorrectly this does not reflect on the
value of my decision-making center. It is still intact, pure,
and of value because it functions to choose between two
paths — good and bad. I happened to send out negative energy from my decision making center and made a mistake, I
transgressed. The problem was that the energy emanating
from my decision center was misguided. My core, my essence — my decision-making soul itself — is untainted. I am
not a naughty boy. What I did was naughty. If I maintain a
proper perspective on the exercise of my free will then I
need not get depressed as a result of my failing. It was a failing, but I am not a failure. I take responsibility for my failing
as I hit my heart and say: "*Ki chatanu* — For we (I) have
strayed."

I can repair the damage caused to others, and thereby
to God's world, by redirecting my spiritual energy from my
decision making center in order to create positive spiritual
energy in the form of a mitzvah the next time I am faced
with the same choice. Thus, I am still in control of my decision making process. This instills me with a sense of hope
that I can improve my behavior.

ראה בענינו
Personal Effort

My mother always told me: "God helps those who
help themselves." It is given that I am not permit-
ted to sit back with my arms folded and have God
arrange a wife or a job for me. Rather, I work in partnership

with God. I must do my best, and the "Boss" will do the rest. As the Talmud tells us: "One doesn't rely on miracles."[20] I must put in my *"hishtadlus,"* my effort, and Hashem will guide me along the path.

This concept is beautifully illustrated by one of the principles derived from the miracle of Chanukah. The Maccabees found enough oil to last naturally for one day. Miraculously, the oil lasted eight days instead of one. The Beis Yosef, Rabbi Yosef Karo, the compiler of the *Shulchan Aruch*, asks a famous question: If the miracle was that the oil lasted an additional seven days, then why do we celebrate Chanukah for eight days? Wasn't the first day natural, thereby necessitating a seven-day holiday to celebrate the supernatural seven days?

One of the most beautiful answers to the Beis Yosef's question is as follows:

When we light the Chanukah candles we are not only celebrating the miracle of the supernatural. We are also celebrating the phenomenon of the natural being transformed into the supernatural. We are celebrating the moment when our effort in finding one cruse of oil which should have lasted one day is taken by Hashem and transported into the realm of the supernatural by lasting a further seven days. In its totality, then, we are celebrating a partnership — our act of faith in God and His taking that faith and lighting the darkness for us. That is why we celebrate for eight days. The first candle represents our human effort. When we take the first step and initiate a relationship with Hashem then He will respond by taking our spiritual energy into another dimension.

When I ask God to fight my battles with the words

"*Rivah riveinu* — Take up our grievance," I am not asking Him to do all the fighting for me. Rather, I am asking Him to help me clarify which are the crucial battles that I should engage in. I have to draw my battle lines with a sense of priority. Which are the central battles and challenges that I was put here to meet?

Let us trace the words "*rivah riveinu*" to their spiritual source in Tehillim: "*Rivah rivi u'gealeini, l'imrascha chayeini* — Fight my battle and redeem me for the sake of Your words.[21] The Radak comments on this verse: "*L'imrascha*, for the sake of your words: meaning, to follow Your word I request life, and I do not request life merely to enjoy the pleasures of the world."

In essence, I am saying: "God — You are my Chief of Staff. Please grant me the insight to plan my life's strategy with wisdom." This implies that I have a God-given mission to achieve during my lifetime. I have been given my marching orders from God Himself. Three times a day during my morning, afternoon, and evening prayers I report back to my Commanding Officer to ask for clarification of the current state of affairs on the battlefront. Thus, this *berachah* ends with the words: "*Go'el Yisrael* — Redeemer of Israel," in the present tense. When I ask God for insight as to where to concentrate my efforts, it causes me to introspect and clarify in my own mind those which are my priority challenges.

רפאנו ה' ונרפא
Healthy Living

When I meet people who are experiencing financial problems or other material difficulties, they will often say to me: "As long as I have my health — that's the most important thing."

We've all said this at one time or another. I have said it myself many times. But do I really mean it, or do I just resort to it as a rationalization when the material aspects of my life are not going well? If my health was the most important thing then shouldn't it be referred to daily? In this *berachah* of *Refa'enu* I put my money where my health is, and I pray for health even before the blessing for livelihood!

This petition for health compels me to contemplate my health as something which is not dependent on me, but God. Of course, I have to exercise, eat properly, and refrain from taking drugs which will harm me, but the involuntary functions of my body organs and systems depend ultimately on God. According to Etz Yosef this is referred to in the words: *"V'haaleh refuah sheleimah l'chol makoseinu* — Bring *complete* recovery to all our ailments."

Being aware of the precariousness of my physical condition urges me into a relationship with my ultimate Doctor, the Almighty, as the Torah states: "I am God your Healer."[22]

There is also a spiritual health that I seek in this *berachah*. The Iyun Tefillah states that: *"l'chol makoseinu"* ("for all our ailments") means: "whether physical ailments or spiritual turmoil."

This hints at that interconnection and interdependence of physical and spiritual well-being. The medical world today readily recognizes a spiritual "will to live" as an important factor in a patient's recovery.

When I ask God to heal me physically I must ask for a *"refuah sheleimah,"* a complete recovery, since my physical recovery is completely up to God. However, when it comes to my spiritual well-being, the Etz Yosef suggests that the opening words of this *berachah*, *"Refa'enu Hashem* — Heal us, O God,"* refer to Hashem *beginning* the process of my spiritual health by having planted within me a yearning to be close to Him. The next word, *"v'nerafei* — and we will be healed"* is in the plural, which means that I can take the spirituality that God has given me and cause my spiritual self to blossom and flourish. The plural, *"v'nerafei,"* means that God and I, in partnership, contribute jointly to my spiritual well-being, even though the "healing" itself comes solely as a gift from God. I must personally invest energy and effort in my spiritual growth, but it is God alone who grants me the reward of spiritual health.

When I ask Hashem for physical and spiritual health I can imagine Him wanting to know why I want it. "If I grant you health," I imagine God saying, "what are you going to use it for?" My answer is found in the words of this *berachah*: *"Ki Sehilasenu Atah* — for You are our praise."* I ask for health, not for my own sake, but for Your sake, Hashem. I want to serve You, and I can better further Your goals and values if I am well.[23]

If I am asking Hashem for well-being in order to serve Him, what happens if I am feeling less than well? Doesn't my self-esteem suffer a blow if I am unable to fulfill my purpose of learning Torah, davening, fulfilling mitzvos, and doing *chesed*? The answer, relates Rabbi Abraham Twerski,[24] is that God only asks me to serve Him in accordance with the best of my abilities at this particular moment. If at present I am unwell, I must still strive to do the best I can having regard to my current limitations. God does not expect from me more than I can deliver. Thus, I can still maintain my

sense of worth and self-esteem as long as I am doing the best
I can for God, having regard to the circumstances with
which He is challenging me. In fact, that perhaps is the test
— to continue serving Hashem despite my limitations. In
other words, "go with what you've got." When I am well, I
ask God to continue my good health so that I can continue to
work for Him. When I am unwell, I can still maintain my
self-esteem by serving God with my "best shot" under the
circumstances, while asking God to restore me to good
health so that I can be even more effective in His service.

An important indicator of my self-esteem is my willingness to think beyond my own needs. This is the reason that
each of the thirteen middle prayers in the *Amidah* are
rendered in the plural. This *berachah* says "*Refa'enu —
Heal us*" because we include all those who are ill in our
prayers.

When Avraham and Sarah were unable to conceive,
there was an incident where Sarah was abducted by
Avimelech, and Avimelech and his countrymen were punished with barrenness. Praying for someone else increases
sensitivity and expands our personality. We become transformed and in the process become deserving of a new judgment ourselves. Avraham prayed for their recovery,[25] and
they were healed. The next verse in the Torah states, "And
God remembered Sarah and she conceived." Rashi comments as follows:

> This section [of Sarah conceiving] follows immedi-
> ately after the section of the recovery of
> Avimelech's countrymen, to teach us that anyone
> who requests mercy for his friend, where he

himself is in need of the same mercy, he will be answered first.[26]

Sarah had conceived before Avimelech's people were healed as a result of Avraham's prayer for others, while Avraham's own wife was also in need of a recovery from barrenness. Praying for someone else increases our sensitivity — and expands our personality. We became transformed and in the process become deserving of a new judgment ourselves.

ברך עלינו
Someone Has to Win the Lottery — Why Can't It Be Me?

This blessing is a plea for *parnasah* — livelihood. Each of us, including me, has at least once, secretly prayed: "Dear God — please let me win the lottery!"

Imagine God hearing this heartfelt prayer. What would God respond? He would say: "My dear child, what are you planning to do with the money?"

I might answer: "I will retire early, buy a house in France, travel around the world, and give to charity."

God would say: "And what about Me? What do you plan to do to advance My plans, My goals, My standards?"

I might respond: "But I said I would give to charity. Isn't that advancing Your standards?"

God might say: "I want you to give yourself to charity. How many charity projects are you going to establish? Are you going to involve yourself in these charitable activities? I don't only want you to give to charity, I want you to transform yourself into a charitable human being. I want you to dedicate yourself, your being, to Me. That's why I put you in My world because I know you can achieve great things for My people and My world. I am giving you this money as a trustee, the beneficiary being those over whom you have jurisdiction — your family, your corner of the community. Now that I have given you my lottery contribution, I want you to contribute *yourself* to others."

Therefore, when I pray for *parnasah* I must pray in the words of this *berachah*: "*V'es kol minei tevuasah l'tovah* — and all its kinds of crops for the best." The Iyun Tefillah explains that wealth can be a test. Wealth may turn my head and I may choose to indulge in my own pleasures and desires. I must therefore pray that my wealth is used *"l'tovah"* — for goodness.

The Talmud says, *"Ein tov elah Torah* — there is no goodness other than Torah."[27] This means that I must learn to use my wealth and livelihood to further spiritual Torah values — including a Jewish education for my children, furthering my own spiritual development, community and charity work, and founding community projects — thus making myself into a *kli*, a receptacle of *berachah*, which in turn can be used to serve Hashem. My life would then take on more meaning and value in the eyes of Hashem, thus elevating my self-worth and self-perception as a person who dedicates himself to purposeful and worthwhile endeavors.

תקע בשופר גדול
At One with Myself

If I am spiritually motivated, my body is more likely to respond than if I am down or depressed. This *berachah* refers to this type of spiritual well-being and contentment when I say that I seek God's help to bring about *cheruseinu* — our freedom. This freedom is not only referring to national redemption but according to Avudraham it refers also to a personal freedom or redemption from my challenges and problems.

The greatest challenge of spiritual freedom is to attain mastery over my desires and emotions — basically over my "self." This is a life-long task. Sometimes my mind wanders from my intended task or endeavor. Sometimes my impulses or desires cause me to seek physical pleasure when I should be seeking spiritual pleasure. For example, as I walk by a non-kosher restaurant, the physical drive to satisfy the desire of my taste buds may cause me to lust after a cheeseburger. I have to conduct a spiritual check of my "pleasure principle" as to whether I should act upon this physical instinctive desire. I check the Torah yardstick: "Thou shalt not seethe a kid in its mother's milk,"[28] and find that although I would like to have this cheeseburger, it is not kosher and would not therefore be healthy for my *neshamah*. Thus, I must cause my spiritual value system to control my physical drives. I channel my physical drives into a closer relationship with God by encouraging myself to follow His will as set out in the Torah.

Is that all I get? A spiritual pat on the back for following the Torah instead of giving into my lust for physical gratification? It seems very difficult to quantify or fully appreciate this spiritual accomplishment when I have sacrificed a lifetime of delicious cheeseburgers. Sometimes I wish I would get more "return" for "investing" in this spiritual path.

But I do get more. I have only to be aware of the benefits and allow the spiritual "freedom" I have accomplished

to translate itself into a physical feeling of inspiration —
which is even more pleasurable than the cheeseburger I
have given up. The moment I walk by the restaurant, or give
up some other personal vice, like smoking, looking where I
shouldn't look, or eating that extra piece of chocolate
mousse cake (when I am on a diet), I feel spiritually uplifted,
which causes my body to become physically energized in
that I won this mini-battle with my physical drives. The re-
sulting physical surge of adrenalin that arises out of my spiritual victory, is a physical "high."

When I say the words *"V'kabetzeinu yachad me'arba
kanfos ha'aretz* — Gather us together from the four corners
of the earth," I am not only praying for the ingathering of
the exiles from "the four corners of the earth" prior to the
coming of *Mashiach*. I am also praying for the ingathering
of my "self" as I may find myself sometimes drawn to the
four corners of "earthiness" — the physical in me as I follow
paths of secular thought, Western values, physical drives,
and egocentrism. These temptations tend to "exile" me into
a personal diaspora — away from my ultimate destiny. I am
praying to return from the four corners of my exile to my
"yachad" — my *"echad,"* my singularity, which is my unique
contribution to the Jewish world. Once I hear the shofar,
i.e., an inspiring lecture, an inspiring *shacharis* service, or a
spiritual high in performing a mitzvah, it acts as a catalyst
for me to return to my real "self" — to be personally
"yachad" or "one" with myself in pursuit of my mission of
serving God by following *ratzon Hashem* — the will of God.

על הצדיקים
I'm Okay

When I was contemplating leaving my law practice I attended a Purim Seudah in Toronto at the home of the late Rabbi Dovid Kalman Drebin, *z"l*. One of his students, a friend of mine, Rabbi Danny Eisen, *shlita*, who now lives in Israel, delivered a *dvar Torah* which made a profound impression on me. He quoted the *Zohar*[29] on the words: "*Mipnei saivah takum* — In the presence of an old person you shall rise." Rabbi Eisen said that the word "*mipnei*" usually means "in front of" or "in the presence of." It also connotes the idea of alacrity or zeal, as it is related to the word "*lifnei*" — which means "prior to" or "before." Now, said Rabbi Eisen, with this interpretation, let us re-read the verse by placing a comma after the word "*saivah*," an old person, as follows: "*Lifnei saivah, takum* — Before you become an old person, arise."

When I spoke to my wife late that night, I said to her that I could imagine us turning to each other in our eighties and lamenting that we had not had the courage to take the risk of going to Israel to follow our dream. "If we only had the chance to do it again," I imagined myself saying, "things would have been a lot different. I wish I had the guts to 'adventure' life." Before we get old let's arise — and do something with our lives. Instead of life happening to me I can make myself happen to life. And so, we made plans to seek our spiritual future, and we moved to Israel to follow our dream.

If I look back on that decision-making process, I wonder where the "inner strength" came from. From where within my being did I draw the inspiration to make such a risky but exhilarating move? The answer lies in the words of this *berachah* of the *Amidah*. "*Al hatzaddikim v'al hachasidim...yehemu rachamecha* — On the righteous and on the devout...may Your compassion be aroused."

There is a portion of my psyche and being which is tzaddik-like — "righteous." It is the spark of Godliness in me that was implanted in me by God at Mount Sinai. As the Talmud[30] states: "An Israelite, even if he sins, is still an Israelite."

There is an innate goodness in me that yearns for righteousness and is drawn toward sanctity. Sometimes it becomes covered by layers of secularism, materialism, and Western values. It is this blessing, when I stand in self-analysis and self-evaluation before God, that can allow me the spiritual opportunity to locate the righteousness within my soul — and to activate it.

Avudraham states that "*al hatzaddikim*" refers to those who are completely righteous. What if I fail to activate the innate righteousness within me and fail to follow God's will? Then I have a second opportunity by virtue of the words "*al hachasidim*," which, according to Avudraham, refers to *ba'alei teshuvah* — those who "return" to a Torah way of life. There is within me a spark of Jewishness which wants me to return to a Torah way of life. It resides within each of us.

The *berachah* of the *Amidah* goes on to ask God: "*V'sim chelkeinu imahem* — and place our lot with them." My *chelek* (portion) in the Divine Plan is there waiting to be activated and achieved. I end this *berachah* with a request that Hashem grant me assistance in activating the righteousness within me: "*Baruch Atah Hashem, Mishan u'Mivtach latzaddikim* — Blessed are You, God, the Mainstay and Assurance of the righteous."

The Talmud states: "A person who seeks purity will be assisted in his quest."[31] I must realize, however, that in this spiritual pursuit I can only succeed if I ask God to help me cut through my physical outer layers into my spiritual core.

ולירושלים עירך
Building Jerusalem

Jerusalem is a city like no other. When I visit the Western Wall and touch its weathered face, I feel its pain, I hear the sigh. When I visit Meah Shearim, I get the feeling that I was born in a house on one of its narrow, enchanting streets. When I get off a bus on Friday afternoon and the non-religious bus driver says *"Shabbat Shalom,"* I feel a surge of hope for the Jewish future.

When I say the words of this *berachah* in the distant land of Diaspora England, I feel very far from the wonder that is Jerusalem. What real connection do I have to the holy city? How do I have the chutzpah to ask God: "May You rebuild it soon in our days as an eternal structure"?

If I am asking God to rebuild the city, I could imagine Him saying to me: "And what are you doing to help rebuild Jerusalem?"

The midrash states:

> In truth the wall of fire that God will cause to descend with the completed [pre-built] third Holy Temple in Jerusalem is presently being created by the fiery sparks of awe that servants of God create when they learn Torah; and in their service of God the Almighty joins the sparks together, and from

there He creates the holy wall of fire.[32]

Thus, I do have a role to play in the rebuilding of the Temple. The return of God's *Shechinah* to Jerusalem is an ongoing process. The fact that this *berachah* begins with the Hebrew letter "*vav*," which means "and," indicates that if I bring out my unique contribution of *adding* my spark of fire to the wall of spiritual fire, this will help bring about *Yerushalayim Habenuyah* — the rebuilt Jerusalem.

את צמח דוד
God Listens

I am always fascinated to hear what the catalyst was that "turned on" a particular person to Torah Judaism. I recently heard about a young man who had been a "once a year" Jew. He was in the synagogue on *Kol Nidre* night, and Rabbi Shlomo Levin, a dynamic leader who has revived the community of South Hampstead in London, suggested that the congregants open their hearts and tell God what they feel, because "God is interested in what you have to say." The young man was moved and shocked. He never heard anyone say that God actually listened to him. He spoke his heart to God that *Kol Nidre* night. The young man is now *shomer Torah u'mitzvos* (observant).

When I pray I must admit that sometimes the words float out into space without being directed toward God. I believe the reason is that I don't really feel that God has cause to listen to me. If only I could imagine God "standing" in front of me and my conversing with Him, my prayers would become more "real."

God is not a concept. He is a reality. He is the Source of my existence. The only way I could imagine Him listening to

me is if I had something of value to say. I do. I offer myself —
my being — to God. I know I have value because He instilled
that value in me. Just as a parent brings a child into the
world and then enters into a relationship with this child, so
too God, the Source of all life, gives me life and offers me a
relationship. I would only be motivated to take God up on
His offer of a relationship if I felt that I was valuable in His
eyes.

Thus, in this *berachah* I pray to God: "For Your redemption we have hoped." The very fact that I am asking for
Hashem's redemption helps make me worthy of His redemption. I ask God to save me in His chosen fashion — I
say "*l'yishuascha*," for Your redemption of me. This means
that God has a particular, unique redemption set aside and
hand picked just for me. I may pray that God save me from
my financial worries by allowing me to win the lottery, but
God may have His own redemption plan in mind for me.
When I pray for *Your* redemption, not *my* redemption, I am
submitting my will to His. I turn to God: This is what I feel I
need — but if You, God, feel it is not right for me, please
don't give it to me." Far from being a belittling experience —
by giving up that which I feel is necessary to whatever God
feels is right for me — this can be a transcendent moment.
This is the moment I say to God: I am of value to Your world
and to You, God. I am worthy of your assistance, guidance,
and deliverance. Please redeem me.

שמע קולנו
Prayer as Chutzpah

As a Canadian living in England I hardly ever have
to identify myself when I say "hello" o   n the

telephone. The other party hears my Canadian accent and immediately says: "Hello Rabbi Roll." They identify me by my voice. The voice is the medium which carries the communication. It has a distinct texture and quality which is unique to the speaker. I may say the same words as someone else but I am distinct from everyone else because of my *kol* — my voice. Perhaps this is the deeper reason why a *niggun* — a melody without words — is such a popular medium of Jewish song. In a *niggun* I use only my voice — without separating my sounds into words and syllables. My voice emanates from my inner feelings and yearnings. My voice is closer to my real inner self than are my words.

That is why, when Hashem tells Avraham to listen to Sarah when she counsels removing Yishmael from their home, Hashem says: "*Shema b'kolah* — Heed her voice."[33] Rashi comments that the word "*kol*" refers to prophecy: "Sarah was greater than Avraham in prophecy." The Sifsei Chachamim explains that the verse does not say "*Shema l'dvara* — listen to her words," rather "*b'kolah*," which indicates that the voice carries with it a higher level of clarity and truth than do words themselves. This last of the thirteen middle blessings of the *Amidah* beseeches God that He listen to my inner yearnings, my sense of truth, my "voice" — as I say "*Shema koleinu* — Hear our voices."

When Yaakov came before Yitzchak dressed in goat skins so that he would resemble his brother Esav's hairy body, Yitzchak said: "The voice is the voice of Yaakov — the hands are the hands of Esav."[34]

Rabbi Samson Rafael Hirsch comments that Yaakov's "voice" is his inner moral and ethical standard. Yaakov uses his "voice" to guide his life, whereas Esav uses his "hands" — his might, the power of the sword. If I can get in touch with God's standard of truth by being in touch with my inner voice, I can activate my soul and come closer to my Creator.

It is permissible in this *berachah* to add my own personal prayers and requests over and above the formula of the blessing given to us by the *Anshei Knesses HaGadol*. Immediately before the words *"Ki Atah shomea tefillas amcha Yisrael b'rachamim* — Because You listen to the prayers of Your people Yisrael in mercy,"* I can insert my own unique requests.

The Anaf Yosef states:

> It is correct and worthwhile for every person to pray every day for his needs, his livelihood, and that the Torah will not leave the mouths of his children and grandchildren, and that all of his offspring should be true servants of God. If he needs to make a *shidduch* for a child, or to succeed in business, he should pray that God grant him success and that He guide him in the way of truth.

My circumstances, namely family, financial, physical, and spiritual, are unlike those of anyone else. My particular needs are unique and are thus "novel" in the eyes of God. Not only can I pray for my own unique redemption but I *must* pray, otherwise my unique voice will be missing from the world's symphony of yearnings before God.

How do I know God wants to hear from me? Isn't it somewhat "chutzpadik" of me to purport to tell God what I need? Since God is omniscient, He obviously knows my particular needs and circumstances, so why should I have to tell Him? Furthermore, if I have to ask for something, doesn't this imply that I am trying to change God's mind after He decided not to grant me my request?

There is a Torah precedent for man being allowed, in fact invited, to make requests of Hashem. When God was about to destroy Sodom and Gemorrah, Hashem said: "Shall I conceal from Avraham what I do now, now that Avraham is surely to become a great and mighty nation and all the nations of the earth shall bless themselves by him?"[35]

Hashem then proceeded to tell Avraham: Because the outcry of Sodom and Gemorrah has become great, and because their sin has been very grave, I will descend and see: if they act in accordance with its outcry — then destruction! And if not, I will know."

Avraham then proceeded to enter into the first plea bargain in history. Avraham came forward and said:

> Will You also stamp out the righteous with the wicked? What if there should be fifty righteous people in the city? Would You still stamp it out rather than spare the place for the sake of the fifty righteous people in it? It would be sacrilege to You to do such a thing, to bring death upon the righteous along with the wicked; letting the righteous and the wicked fare alike. It would be sacrilege to You! Shall the Judge of all the earth not do justice?

How could Avraham have the chutzpah to challenge God's plans and wisdom? How could he suggest saving Sodom when God already advised him He was going to destroy it? Was he trying to change God's mind? The answer lies not in Avraham's actions but in the words of God. It was Hashem Himself who invited Avraham to tell Him what he thought about God's plan, as the Torah states: "Shall I conceal from Avraham what I do now...."

Why would God tell Avraham about the impending destruction of Sodom if He didn't want Avraham's opinion? Not only did God want to hear from Avraham but He wanted Avraham's input into the decision-making process. Thus, we can say that Avraham acted as God's "partner," providing God with his opinion. It is not that God only has a Heavenly perspective and "needs" an earthly perspective; rather, God wants man to engage Him in dialogue and to create a relationship with Him.

This section of the Torah provides a precedent for God allowing and encouraging me to pray to Him and to ask Him to assist me in my daily needs. Am I trying to change God's mind if He has other plans for me? No. I am trying to change myself by connecting myself to God and His values. Thus, the prayers attract a different plan from God because of my changed values that have arisen through the prayer process.[36]

מודים אנחנו לך
My Personal Relationship with God

We live simultaneously in a two-track system. The first track is the "natural track." In this pathway, statistics rule. If I have an illness in which nine out of ten people statistically die, then I have a one in ten chance of surviving. If statistically one in six new businesses will thrive, then my chance of success is one in six. Simultaneously, there exists a track which takes me beyond the natural law of statistics into the world wherein I am asking Him to "Personally" guide my destiny. This is known as the "supernatural track." While God may still deny my specific request, prayers always work because the act of prayer itself elevates me to this new track — a closer relationship with God.

In the middle of this *berachah* of *Modim*, thanksgiving, which is the concluding section of the *Amidah*, I thank God for allowing me to rise above the natural track, as I say: *"V'al nisecha shebechol yom imanu* — For Your miracles that are with us every day," which alludes to the two-track system. While I can live my life on the statistical, natural, everyday level, I can also choose to reach out and above this track to the level of: *"Va'al nisecha* — for Your miracles."

I don't pray merely in order to move from the natural track to the supernatural, rather I pray to engage God in a personal relationship. God places me in a position of physical and spiritual need so that I can turn to Him and receive the ultimate blessing — a relationship with God Himself. A relationship is a two-way street: it presupposes a party of the first part and a party of the second part. If I, as the party of the second part, receive blessings from Hashem, as Party of the First Part, then I must be of substance and value in God's eyes — an entity worth receiving from Him.

תחנון
Go On, Have a Good Cry

When I feel a wave of emotional pain or despair growing within me, I know that the best way to release that pain is to have a good cry. Crying leaves me in a state of serene and exhausted tranquility.

Why? A person cries because he is disoriented — the status quo has been upset and he is unsure of his footing. His security has been challenged and his confidence has been shaken. If a person fails in a test or project, if he has been emotionally hurt, or if a loved one dies — his status quo has been shaken, he is confused, and he cries. But after the outpouring of emotion — a catharsis — the person reorients himself and begins the process of readjusting to the new set of circumstances; hence the sense of serenity.

When I put my head down on my arm during *Tachanun*, following the *Amidah*, I say:

בְּדִמְעָתִי עַרְשִׂי אַמְסֶה...סוּרוּ מִמֶּנִּי כָּל פֹּעֲלֵי אָוֶן, כִּי שָׁמַע ה' קוֹל בִּכְיִי.

I drench my bed with my tears... Depart from me all evildoers, for Hashem has heard the sound of my weeping.

I am overcome with emotion and I feel like crying. Although God hasn't changed because of my petitions and my cleaving to Him, my old standards, my status quo, has changed. I am a new person for having engaged my Creator in dialogue and having dedicated myself to the standards and values enumerated in the *Amidah*, our relationship is strengthened. But it is a new relationship; I have left the old "me" behind. My old desires and values are no longer. I have been elevated to a new level.

This process scares me. I have urged myself during the *Amidah* to take on new responsibilities and I now must live up to the new "me." The emotional response I feel is one of crying, unsure of my new footing, and so I fall on my arm before God and I ask Him to revoke my old decree — because I have now become a new person and a new decree is in order. With my change in values comes an emotional outpouring — I cry. This moment of emotional catharsis is a crucial moment of self-awareness. I am moving from one spiritual level to the next and I am in an emotional state of flux. I can turn only to God for assistance as I place my head in my arm, which symbolically means that I place my destiny in His hands. As King David states: "Cast upon Hashem your burden and He will sustain You."[37]

This moment of insecurity and disorientation dissipates in my placing myself in total submission before God. I place my "self" — the metamorphosis from the "old me" to the "new me" — into God's hands. My old self merges with my new self, through my encounter with God. I become aware of my "self" from the midst of my *aliyah*, my elevation. The transformation of my self is the real me.

NOTES

1. *Berachos* 32b.
2. *Siach Tzvi, Amidah*.
3. Bereishis 32:10.
4. Ibid. 32:29.
5. The letters Y-I-S-R-A-E-L can also spell the words *"yasher-El,"* which mean God is straight (true). It also means that Israel reflects the straight and direct hand or Providence of God.
6. Rabbi Pesach Oratz, Jerusalem.
7. *Nesivos Shalom, Parashas Vayishlach*. The name "Yaakov" represents service of Hashem *mi'yirah*, awe, while the name "Yisrael" represents service of Hashem *me'ahavah*, love. Yaakov struggled with the "angel" and grew in his *avodas Hashem* from awe of God

— his Yaakov self into his higher self: Yisrael.

8. *Mishnah Berurah*, commenting on the meaning of the *berachah* as explained by the *Shulchan Aruch, Orach Chaim* 115.

9. *Sha'ar Rishon, Yediah u'Bechirah.*

10. Yirmiyahu 9:23.

11. *Tiferes Yisrael, Parashas Pinchas*, by Yisroel Charif of Satanov. When the Torah says, "And it was on that day that he entered the house to do his work..." Rashi comments: " 'To do his work' means to have relations with her [Potiphar's wife] but he did not because the image of his father's face appeared to him in the window" (*Sotah* 36b). Yisroel Charif of Satanov comments that the image of "his father" means that he could not bring himself to sin because he saw his "*av*" — his father — his source which is rooted in the *sefirah* of "*chesed*." *Chesed* is true giving, true love. Misguided *chesed* leads to sexual immorality.

12. *Niddah* 30b.

13. Tatz, *Living Inspired*, p. 24.

14. Devarim 33:4.

15. Ibid. 29:14.

16. *Yoma* 73b.

17. Rabbi Mayer Schiller, *The Road Back* (Jerusalem: Feldheim Publishers, 1978), 144.

18. According to Rav Eliyahu Dessler in *Michtav MiEliyahu*, vol. 1, pp. 103–104, man moves through time in a spiral. Every Shabbos I re-enter the spiritual zone of the first Shabbos of creation. Every Pesach I re-enter the spiritual zone of freedom from Egypt, etc.

19. Abraham Twerski, *Self Improvement — I'm Jewish* (New York: Sha'ar Press, 1995), 43, 84.

20. *Pesachim* 64b.

21. Tehillim 119:154.

22. Shemos 15:26.

23. Rabbi Uziel Milevski, *z"l*, Jerusalem.

24. *Let Us Make Man*, p. 115.

25. Bereishis 20:17.

26. Ibid. 21:1.

27. *Berachos* 5a.

28. Shemos 23:19.

29. *Zohar*, Vayikra 19:32.

30. *Sanhedrin* 44a.
31. *Shabbos* 104a.
32. Dover Shalom, quoting the Sifri.
33. Bereishis 21:12.
34. Ibid. 27:22.
35. Ibid. 18:17.
36. Gottlieb, *The Informed Soul*, pp. 164–180.
37. Tehillim 55:23.

Chapter 5

CONCLUDING PRAYERS

אשרי
Where on Earth Is the World to Come?

The Jew is a time traveler. When I perform a mitzvah I travel back in time to shake hands with the heritage of my ancestors. I simultaneously travel forward in time as I ensure the continuity of Jewish practice in my children by serving as a role model for them to emulate. I live in the past, present, and future at the same time. With the saying of Ashrei I am able to praise God in this world and simultaneously transport myself into the World to Come. This is what is meant by the statement in the Gemara: "Anyone who says *Ashrei* three times a day is assured that he will be a child of the World to Come."[1] *Ashrei* is the Jewish time machine.

The Hebrew term for a "child of the World to Come" is *"ben olam haba"* — which means that he or she is assured of a place in the next world. Every line of Ashrei begins with another letter of the Hebrew alphabet. When I praise God with every letter of the alphabet, i.e., with every thought and deed, I am creating a spiritual energy that I will "live in" and enjoy in the World to Come. The Nefesh Hachaim[2] asks the age-old question: "Where on earth is the World to Come?" He answers that the World to Come is right here *in this world*. The spiritual energy I create through the performance of the mitzvos is presently building my spiritual World to Come dimension, within this world. Thus, I can live in this world and simultaneously be a "child of the World to Come."

Living in this world while being conscious of my future — my World to Come — is crucial to my self-esteem. It reminds me that I have a future. It reinforces the realization that I have a purpose and that my life is "going somewhere."

One of the components of the negative self-image is that of despair — that all is lost, there is no hope for tomorrow. Realizing, however, that each act I do now is actually creating for myself a positive future — my World to Come — can counteract this emotional despair. My prayers to God, despite my difficult personal situation, can transport me beyond my crisis. By praying to God, I have created a reality that lives beyond my current difficulty. The very act of prayer itself propels me over the hurdle that I am currently facing. I can literally "laugh in the face of adversity" because I am already beyond the adversity, as a "child of the World to Come."

When Moshe asked God which name He should be known as, Hashem answered, "I will be what I will be."[3]

Why did Hashem reveal himself in the future tense? Rashi answers: To teach us that He will be with us in all future exiles. The essence of the belief in God is a belief that I have a future. The belief that I am a child of the World to Come is a belief that my future is guided and protected by the *"Boreh u'Manhig"* — the Creator and the Guide of history.

למנצח מזמור לדוד
How to Acquire Self-Esteem?

People always tell me: "You've got to have self-confidence. You've got to believe in yourself!" The problem is, however, that if I don't have self-confidence and I don't believe in myself, how do I acquire it? Where can I buy some self-esteem? Tell me and I'll buy it in bulk. I have a negative self-image precisely because I don't believe I am of value and worth. Telling me to believe in myself just isn't enough. You've got to tell me *why* I should believe in myself.

When I ask God to intervene in my life I am asking the King of kings to take time out of His busy schedule dealing with peace negotiations in Israel, ethnic cleansing in the Balkans, and state sponsored terrorism, to deal with my personal problems. The very fact that I pray to God as the only One who has the ability to assist me, allows me to presume that God has the time for me. With this realization I can turn to Hashem and ask Him in the words of this psalm, *"Yishlach ezrecha miKodesh* — Send me help from the Sanctuary."

I am worthy of Hashem's holy assistance because I carry within me a spark of Godliness. I can take the God-given *neshamah* within me and elevate it to an even higher level of *kedushah* by the exercise of my free will. If I involve myself in meaningful activities, such as learning Torah and acts of *chesed* and community work, then I can put myself onto God's spiritual frequency and thus be the recipient of His assistance, *"miKodesh"* — from His Sanctuary. This psalm encourages me to continue attracting the positive attention of God by urging myself to stay on a level of *"kodesh,"* which allows Hashem's *berachah* to continue to flow into my spiritual veins.

The bottom line is that ultimately I am responsible for my own self-esteem. I have the God-given foundation of worthiness and therefore can allow myself the gift of seeing myself as a person with value. I have objective worth in God's eyes by being a child of Hashem, which allows me to acquire self-esteem in my own eyes. I can build up my own self-concept and positive self-image by actively putting my God-given soul into "*kedushadik*" (sanctified) circumstances and pursuits which will reinforce my perception of my own value. I cannot hand over responsibility for my self-image to some outside force, person, or authority. I cannot spend my life blaming my parents for failing to create in me a positive self-image. I must take personal charge of my own self-esteem by appreciating my own God-given sanctity and by building upon it — through the exercise of my free will. Then I can feel as if I have had personal input in developing my own "self" by virtue of my involvement in meaningful projects and activities.

If, after trying to activate my self-esteem for years through courses, discussions with personal advisors, and reading books on self-esteem, I still find myself with a negative self-concept, I must ask myself the following question: What benefit do I get in purposely maintaining a negative view of myself? One of the answers may very well be to elicit sympathy or attention. Perhaps my cognitive process works like this: Whenever life deals me a difficult challenge I naturally switch into the "poor me, negative image, no self-esteem" mode, which, hopefully, will elicit words of encouragement, support, and praise from loved ones and friends. Furthermore, the motivation to maintain a low self-esteem is that it makes me look humble and modest if I fail to believe in myself or if I make out as if my successes are not "so great" after all.

How can I short circuit this roundabout way of getting praise and encouragement? Isn't there a more direct and efficient way of gaining the love and esteem of others? Yes. I learned the method through counseling a young, talented, successful congregant, who thought very poorly of himself despite his tremendous popularity and personal successes. Delving into his childhood we discovered that he had a disciplinarian father and a sensitive mother. Whenever his father would discipline or push him to succeed, his mother would come to his defense and protect his feelings. He learned over time that whenever Dad would scold, demand, and say, "You can do better," all he had to do was to adopt a helpless, "poor me, look how Dad is putting me down" attitude and Mom would come to the rescue with a protective hug and "you're a wonderful child, here's a cookie." So in order to get "the cookie" he learned to adopt a negative self-image. Even though he had left home long ago, he adopted this world view as his own. It was now part of him.

How did this young man learn to break free of the negative self-image syndrome? I pointed out to him that he could bypass the two-step "Dad puts me down, Mom gives me love" (world puts me down, friends give me sympathy) model by introducing God into the equation. Hashem is both Father and Mother. I pointed out to him that God is the One Who, like his father, disciplines and pushes him to better himself, but He is also the One Who, like his mother, comforts and supports him when he falls short of the mark. Here, then, is a reason to let go of the cognitive process which sustains a negative self-image. Let God take over as both Disciplinarian and Protector. Let Hashem encourage you to improve, but allow Him to comfort you if you fail. Cut out the intermediary and go right to the Source. Don't buy retail — go directly to the manufacturer and buy wholesale. As it says in psalm 27, which we read from Rosh Chodesh Elul until Shemini Atzeres: "Though my father and mother have forsaken me, Hashem will gather me in."

In fact, we can allow *Pirkei Avos* to demand from us that we break the negative self-image syndrome, as it states: "...And do not judge yourself to be a wicked person."[4]

If a person sees himself as evil, then it is only one step further to allow himself to slip into a negative lifestyle: a self-fulfilling prophecy. One has to fight the *yetzer hara* which encourages this negative self-image and find the good in oneself in order to perform up to one's potential. I can do this by reminding myself that I have a *yetzer hatov*, as well. We don't hear so much about the *yetzer hatov* because the *yetzer hara* has a better press agent. But I can win this inner battle of wills by concentrating upon and by activating my *yetzer hatov*, which will fill my mind and my psyche with a positive self-image.

ובא לציון גואל
We Will Have Jewish Grandchildren

וּדְבָרַי אֲשֶׁר שַׂמְתִּי בְּפִיךָ, לֹא יָמוּשׁוּ מִפִּיךָ וּמִפִּי זַרְעֲךָ וּמִפִּי זֶרַע
זַרְעֲךָ...

My words that I have placed in your mouth shall not be withdrawn from your mouth, nor

from the mouth of your offspring, nor from the
mouth of your offspring's offspring...

At the 1996 Encounter Conference in London attended by 1500 people, the Chief Rabbi of Israel, Rabbi Yisroel Meir Lau, delivered a moving address. He explained the continuity of Jewish tradition with an anecdote, as follows:

Imagine an Alitalia airplane landing in Rome. An old man comes down the stairs, and one of the workers climbs up.

"What is your name?" asks the airport worker.

The old man, not understanding modern Italian, says three words: *"Veni, Vedi, Veci."*

The worker doesn't understand Latin. An interpreter comes forward.

"Who are you?" asks the worker.

"I am Julius Caesar. Take me to Jupiter's Temple."

"We have no such Temple — but I can take you to the Vatican in Rome."

"Where is the Empire of Rome?"

"We don't rule over any other country," says the airport employee. "We are part of NATO, governed by the United States of America. The Rome of Felini is not the Rome of Caesar."

Now, imagine an Olympic Airline's jet touching down in Athens. A man comes down the stairs and an airport worker climbs up the stairs to help him with his luggage. The man says in Ancient Greek: "My name is Socrates." The airport employee understands only modern Greek. An interpreter arrives on the scene and translates.

Socrates says, "Where is the Temple of Zeus?"

"There is no longer a Temple of Zeus," replies the worker. "We have a Greek Orthodox Church ruling over religious life."

"Take me to the Senate," says Socrates.

"There is no longer a Senate," comes the response.

"Take me to the king of the Empire of Greece."

"There is no longer a king nor a Greek Empire," says the worker. "We don't rule over any other country. We are part of NATO, governed by the United States of America, and we are not the most important part of NATO, at that. The modern Greek government has almost nothing in common with the ancient Greece of Plato and Aristotle; merely geography and some memories. The people are Greek — but the culture of Ancient Greece is no more."

An El Al plane touches down in Ben Gurion Airport in Lod, near Tel-Aviv. Down the stairs comes an old man, who never once visited Israel. One of the workers comes up the stairs, and the old man stretches out his hand and says: *"Shalom Aleichem."* The worker answers immediately: *"Aleichem Shalom!"*

"Who are you?" asks the worker.

"Moshe," says the old man.

"And who are you?"

"Also Moshe, from Tiblisi, in Georgia."

The old man says: "How is it that you still speak the ancient language of Hebrew?"

"I speak only *Ivrit*," says the worker. "I almost forgot my mother tongue of Georgian, since I made aliyah twenty years ago."

Moshe of the Bible was born in Egypt and died in Transjordan. Moshe the airport employee was born in

Tiblisi. Three thousand three hundred years separate the two men named Moshe — and they still speak the same langauge.

Moshe of the Torah says, "I forgot to bring my tallis and tefillin. Where can I buy some?"

"No problem," says the airport worker. "I will lend you mine. There are two synagogues here in the airport terminal — I'll take you there so you can daven *shacharis*. Today is Monday so you can hear the Torah reading."

They are saying the same words today in Ben Gurion International Airport that were sung by Moshe Rabbeinu 3300 years ago. They are wearing the same tallis; the same tefillin; the same language; nothing has changed. Moshe is a *living* person. Our tradition is not out of date. Our tradition is alive.

If and when I teach the words of Jewish tradition to my children, then, and only then, will the words "not be withdrawn from the mouth of your offspring" ring true. Within this obligation of transmitting our ancient and living tradition to the next generation I can find the strength that I seek. God has entrusted me with such an awesome responsibility — obviously He believes I can achieve it. God believes in me. He believes I am equal to the task of transmitting our tradition — a chain of tradition which has been linking generations for thirty-three centuries. And God believes that I am up to the task of keeping it going.

עלינו לשבח
A Greater Version of Myself

אֱמֶת מַלְכֵּנוּ, אֶפֶס זוּלָתוֹ...

True is our King, there is nothing besides Him...

Pirkei Avos[5] states: "Nullify your will before His Will." I give up my will to God by channeling that which I want into what God wants. When I give up my will I am *mevatel*, I sublimate my decision-making in His favor. But this does not mean that I am left with nothing. I have given God my hopes, desires, and intentions but I am maintaining my God-given character, talents, and abilities.

Rabbi Mordechai Gifter[6] states that instead of losing part of my "self" by nullifying or sublimating myself before God, I am actually becoming greater than my own self. A colored chip of stone added to a mosaic simultaneously preserves the identity of the individual stone while integrating it into the organic whole. The colored chip of stone represents the individual — me . When I connect myself to God I am integrating myself with the Mosaic — the Source of Life, Who is Infinite. By so doing I become a greater version of myself. I take on a greater sense of self through my connection to the Infinite.

...כִּי לְךָ תִּכְרַע כָּל בֶּרֶךָ, תִּשָּׁבַע כָּל לָשׁוֹן.

...To You every knee should bend and every tongue should swear.

If I get depressed as a result of a certain crisis or problem, then I am really denying God Himself. He has given me certain personal qualities and strengths that I am asked to use in His Service. If I get "down" because of certain circumstances or difficulties, I am, in essence, arguing with God and in effect saying to Him: "You have made a mistake,

God. You think You gave me strength and abilities to use to deal with this problem, but You were wrong. You didn't give me the right or sufficient abilities to weather this crisis."

If I use my God-given abilities to serve Him, I have achieved personal growth. To be depressed or angry with God because of a certain issue with which He challenges me is to stay static and to fail to actualize my potential. I can maintain self-esteem in the face of adversity when I use my best efforts and talents to deal with the issue at hand and to grow through the experience.

שיר של יום
My Song

The *Shir Shel Yom* "speaks to me" and challenges me to make each new day count in my journey toward achieving my life purpose. That is why we count each day as "*Hayom yom rishon b'Shabbos* — Today is the first day of the Sabbath," "*Hayom yom sheini b'Shabbos* — Today is the second day of the Sabbath," etc. Each day is not referred to by name, rather by number, in order to remind me to make each day count as I work toward Shabbos — which represents spiritual fulfillment. The "song" I sing each day is my daily contribution toward the actualization of my life's potential, which, in the words of the Friday night *Amidah*, is my "*tachlis ma'aseh bereishis*" — the purpose of my creation.

On a deeper level, the daily *Shir Shel Yom* reminds me that each day is "of Shabbos" and is considered as part of the Shabbos experience itself. In this way each day can be "*shabbosdik*" when I make a conscious effort to have my daily activities contribute to achieving personal growth and development. There can be no "down time" or wasted effort.

There is a famous story told of a small town comprised

of ten Jewish families. Every morning there was a minyan, notwithstanding colds, flus, aches, and pains. One day an eleventh family moved into town — and the next day there was no minyan. Everyone expected someone else to be the tenth man that day.

When there are only ten of us each feels a moral responsibility to do his part and to make up the minyan. That is the attitude I should adopt every day. In fact the *Shulchan Aruch*,[7] states: A person should arrive early in synagogue in order to be counted as part of the original ten (to make up the minyan).

Why does it matter if I form part of the original ten at the minyan? So that I can feel as if I personally contributed to the creation of the *kedushah* of the minyan. My efforts count. I can and do make a difference. It is through my efforts that *kedushah* arrived in the community today.

Each of us can, no must, sing our personal *"Shir Shel Yom"* every day. Each day Hashem wants to hear my song, my contribution to the symphony that is the world. Each day, the *Shir Shel Yom* changes to illustrate that each day's experiences make me into a new person. Each of the events which happens to me serves to mould and transform my character and causes me to sing a new song. My song counts — it matters. I can and I do make a difference.

NOTES

1. *Berachos* 4b.
2. *Sha'ar Alef*, ch. 12.
3. Shemos 3:14.
4. *Avos* 2:18.
5. Ibid. 2:4.

6. *Shir HaShirim* (New York: Mesorah Publications, Ltd., 1977), Foreword, xix.

7. *Orach Chaim* 90:14.

Epilogue

PRAYER AS JEWISH SPIRITUALITY

M̲any people have said to me that they like to express their spirituality "their way." One friend told me that he feels uplifted and spiritual when he paddles a canoe on Saturday on a calm lake and feels the breeze tussle his hair. He said that he feels very close to God when he connects with nature in this way. While I agree that he may feel inspired and uplifted by "communing with God" on the lake, it must be understood that communing with nature without acknowledging God as the Source of nature is *not* what is meant by Jewish spirituality. God has defined and outlined the types of spirituality that He seeks from us. He commands and directs us to experience various emotions and feelings of spirituality. For example:

(1) *"Oneg Shabbos"* — Joy of the Sabbath.[1]

(2) *"V'samachta b'chagecha"* — Be happy on your Festivals.[2]

(3) *"Tachas asher lo avadeta es Hashem Elokecha b'smichah"* — Because you did not serve God in joy."[3]

(4) *"V'ahavta es Hashem Elokecha"* — You shall love the Lord, your God...[4]

These are some of the expressions of spirituality that God has told us will make real and eternal spiritual connections with Him.

I cannot delude myself into thinking that any inspiring feeling that I experience is actually making a connection between my *neshamah* and God. He has placed my *neshamah* within me and instructed me how I can activate the pathways of connection with Him.

While you might think that God is displaying the ultimate "chutzpah" in dictating to me how I should relate to Him, there is a deep lesson here that God is trying to teach me.

God legislates certain emotions, feelings, and thoughts because He has determined that this is how I *ought* to feel. Even if I am not feeling particularly inspired or happy on a particular Yom Tov, by requiring me to feel *"simchas Yom Tov"* (the joy of the Festival), God is saying to me that there is a special Godly "spiritual frequency" on this day, and I am urged by Him to raise myself up to connect with it and to inspire my soul with its spiritual energy. Even though I may not feel emotionally "happy," God is asking my soul to feel *spiritually* happy. Thus, Jewish spirituality is beyond the emotional and psychological. It allows me to get to know a deeper part of myself. Jewish law and custom is the spiritual "soul food" which nourishes my inner being and allows me to taste eternity while I am still in this world.

Prayer is a specific example of this type of Jewish spirituality. Many of my students ask me: "Why can't I pray in my own words whenever I feel God's presence touch me?" Indeed, I can utter my own personal prayer to God at any time and in any dignified, clean place. I can even add my own personal prayer in any language at certain points in the *Amidah*. Prayer, however, is much more than making a connection with God when I feel Him close to me. Prayer in the prescribed formula contained in the Siddur and at set times is an expression of my *ongoing* relationship with God and my desire that He stand by me *always*, not only at those moments when I feel I "need" Him.

The formal prayers do not only express how I feel but how I "ought" to be feeling. I ought to acknowledge the gift of the life force within me every second of the day. For example, as the Yerushalmi states: "Would that a man could pray all day long."[5] I should feel myself in awe of the presence of my Creator at all times, not merely three times a day. I pray at *shacharis, minchah*, and *ma'ariv* as symbolic expressions of my feeling of awe of God always — morning, noon, and night.

May our prayers strengthen our relationship with God and transform us into better *avdei Hashem* — servants of God.

NOTES

1. *Shulchan Aruch, Orach Chaim* 242:1; *Mishnah Berurah*.
2. Devarim 16:14.
3. Ibid. 28:47.
4. Ibid. 6:5.
5. *Talmud Yerushalmi, Shabbos* 1:2.